Spiritual Guides

FRED DALLMAYR

Spiritual Guides

PATHFINDERS IN THE DESERT

University of Notre Dame Press

Notre Dame, Indiana

University of Notre Dame Press
Notre Dame, Indiana 46556
undpress.nd.edu

Published in the United States of America

Library of Congress Cataloging-in-Publication Data

Names: Dallmayr, Fred R. (Fred Reinhard), 1928– author.
Title: Spiritual guides : pathfinders in the desert / Fred Dallmayr.
Description: Notre Dame, Indiana : University of Notre Dame Press, 2017. |
    Includes bibliographical references and index. |
Identifiers: LCCN 2017024327 (print) | LCCN 2017047576 (ebook) | ISBN
    9780268102593 (pdf) | ISBN 9780268102609 (epub) | ISBN 9780268102586
    (hardback) | ISBN 0268102589 (hardcover)
Subjects: LCSH: Spiritual life—Christianity. | Christian life. | Spiritual
    life. | Religious life. | Spirituality. | BISAC: PHILOSOPHY / Ethics &
    Moral Philosophy. | POLITICAL SCIENCE / History & Theory. |
    RELIGION / Spirituality.
Classification: LCC BV4501.3 (ebook) | LCC BV4501.3 .D3523 2017 (print) |
    DDC 230—dc23
LC record available at https://lccn.loc.gov/2017024327

∞ *This paper meets the requirements of ANSI/NISO Z39.48-1992
(Permanence of Paper).*

In Memory of

Rev. Theodore M. Hesburgh, C.S.C. (1917–2015)

and Rev. George F. McLean, O.M.I. (1929–2016)

Everyone who hates his brother is a murderer.
—1 John 3:15

When the practice of ahimsa *becomes universal,*
God will reign on earth as He does in heaven.
—Mahatma Gandhi, *Non-Violence*
in Peace and War (1948)

Come Holy Spirit,
fill the hearts of your
faithful and kindle in them
the fire of your love.
Send forth your Spirit
and they shall be created.
And you shall renew
the face of the earth.
—Pentecostal Chant

Contents

Preface

Reflecting on contemporary religiosity in North America, theologian Matthew Ashley reached some discomforting conclusions. "If one peruses the sections on 'spirituality' or 'inspiration' in a Noble or Border bookstore," he wrote, "one comes away with the impression that spirituality is something that relatively secure middle- or upper-middle-class North Americans do in their spare time." As part of the pervasive culture of consumerism, spirituality appears here as another marketable item designed to relieve a lingering sense of boredom—an item readily supplied by a culture industry that has discovered that "spirituality sells."[1]

The present book is not, and cannot possibly be, a part of the reigning culture industry. This is so because it basically challenges and disrupts the dominant Western culture, seeing it mostly as an expanding wasteland or desert (in the sense of Nietzsche's saying "the desert grows"). This desert character is evident in incessant warmongering, in political and economic domination, in spoliation of natural resources, in destruction of human solidarity, and above all in mindless consumerism and greedy self-satisfaction. Spirituality, as it is treated here, is a painfully wrenching effort to extricate human and social life from these ills. This effort takes the form of engaged practices, but first and most of all of radical mindfulness and contemplation—a contemplation seeking to break through to the depths of existential experience in order to retrieve buried layers of insight as a pathway to recovery.

Spiritual effort in this sense is not, and cannot be, a purely academic exercise or something people may (or may not) do "in their spare time." It can arise only from a profoundly felt need or neediness: the need to escape from the spreading devastation. Martin Heidegger, in his study of Nietzsche, speaks of the mindless or absent-minded "needlessness" (*Notlosigkeit*) of modern culture covering up an urgent existential need (*Not*): "The reigning lack of need renders 'Being' needful in the extreme." As he adds: "Needlessness, as the guise of Being's extreme needfulness, reigns precisely in the age of the darkening of beings, our age of confusion, violence and despair in human culture." What is required for recovery is a thorough exposure to the desert (of needlessness) to experience there the full force of the needed recovery.[2]

What Heidegger states in difficult philosophical language, the spiritual leaders I have chosen to discuss in this book express in a different, more accessible idiom. Nevertheless, at least three of the guides—Paul Tillich, Raimon Panikkar, and Thomas Merton—were thoroughly familiar with Heidegger's work and often cite (directly or indirectly) his teachings. Here I make no claim of a coincidence of views, just the presence of certain affinities. What links all four guides (including Pope Francis) together is the view of spiritual life as an *itinerarium*, a pathway along difficult and often uncharted roads. But this also corresponds to Heidegger's motto, "*Wege nicht Werke*" (Paths not Works).

Pentecostal chant "Come, Holy Spirit," cited in one of the opening epigraphs, was the favorite prayer of Rev. Theodore M. Hesburgh, C.S.C., president of the University of Notre Dame from 1952 to 1987, an exemplary practitioner of what is called "contemplation in action," who welcomed me warmly to Notre Dame in 1979. This book is a memorial tribute to Father Hesburgh and also to Fr. George McLean, who allowed the spirit to guide him in his relentless explorations of cultural and religious traditions around the world.

As always, my deep thanks go to my family and my friends, who have supported and continue to support me on my itinerary.

Introduction

Through the Desert

One of the famous passages in Nietzsche's *Thus Spoke Zarathustra* says that "the desert grows." "Desert" here means a spreading wasteland where everything creative, fruitful, and nourishing decays and withers. It is in this sense that the passage is often invoked by social and political thinkers (including myself)—and for good reasons.[1] Nietzsche's phrase draws attention to a central feature of late-modern life: the growing atrophy of cultural and spiritual legacies and the increasing spoliation and depletion of the natural habitat. The main reason for this decay is the near-exclusive emphasis on productivity, efficiency, and profitability and the transformation of everything valuable into a useful resource (what Martin Heidegger called "standing reserve"). If one adds to these forms of spoliation the expanding arsenal of lethal weapons and the growing capability of humankind to engineer the nuclear destruction of the world, Nietzsche's desert or wasteland becomes an overwhelming picture of doom. I agree with this picture. However, I want to draw attention here to another sense of "desert," curiously related to the first, namely, as a place of solitude, meditation, and recovery from the wasteland of spoliation and devastation. All the great religious and spiritual traditions of the world pay tribute to this kind of desert.

The curious relation of the two senses of "desert" means that one has to venture into an uninhabited, unsettled place or no-place in order to perceive the settled ways of existing society as a wasteland and thereby find recovery. The story of the Jewish exodus from Egypt is a good example. Having been enslaved in Egypt for a generation after the death of Joseph—and having been in many ways assimilated into Egyptian customs and beliefs—the Israelites determined to break free of their slavery under the leadership of Moses. Avoiding hostile territories, Moses led his followers into desert land, which caused them much suffering and deprivation. When they reached the Red Sea, with their enemies in hot pursuit, the sea was miraculously parted and transformed again into dry land. Following this divine rescue, the Israelites began their wandering in the wilderness, a wandering that is said to have lasted for forty years—a period presumably required for them to abandon their Egyptian ways of life. According to scripture, the people in the desert were nourished by "manna" from heaven and water from the rocky ground; at Mount Sinai, they were given divine commandments to guide and restructure their lives. Thus prolonged and difficult desert experiences gave rise to new beginnings. As the psalmist writes (107:35–36): "He turns a desert into pools of water, a parched land into gusting springs. There he lets the hungry dwell, and establish a city to live in."[2]

Jesus retreated frequently into the desert or wilderness for intensive prayer and self-collection. Most memorable is the time, at the beginning of his ministry, when it is said that he was led by the spirit into the wilderness, where he fasted for forty days. At the end of this period, he was tempted by the devil in various ways. The most significant of these in the present context was the temptation of worldly power and domination. The devil, we are told (Luke 4:5–8), took Jesus to a high place, showed him all the kingdoms of the earth, and offered him "all this power and their glory" in exchange for submission. To Jesus, whose only obedience was to God, this clearly was a very bad bargain: to the lover of God, all the kingdoms, with all their power and glory, must have appeared as a vast wasteland—in contemporary terminology, as a desert ravaged by militarism and consumerism. Thus the temptation in this case was not even tempting. Moreover, there is a curious twist to the story: the temptation was actually redundant. For the believer, God already rules the world and "all the kingdoms" and thus already is endowed with all possible authority and glory. Jesus's refusal contains an important lesson for all times: that God rules differently, that his authority is altogether different from worldly power and glory.[3]

Desert and wilderness also play pivotal roles in other religious traditions. Prophet Muhammad, the founder of Islam, is known to have retreated periodically during his middle years into a mountainous wilderness near Mecca in order to pray and meditate. One night around 610 A.D., while praying at Mount Hira, he had a spiritual experience in the sense that (as tradition teaches) the "word of God" was revealed to him by archangel Gabriel—a word that he initially resisted and did not feel competent to disclose to anyone. It was only after a period of self-doubt and repeated prayerful retreats that he accepted his role as a discloser or "reciter" of God's message. His opponents were mainly the rich members of the urban "consumer" society in Mecca. A dramatic exodus from affluent, settled life into "unsettlement" or no-place lies also at the roots of historical Buddhism. As we know, Siddhartha Gautama grew up in wealthy circumstances as the spoiled heir of the Shakya kingdom in Nepal. As a young man, however, he tired of the life of pointless pleasure and "conspicuous consumption" and went forth into "homelessness" (*pravrajya*) with little or nothing. He wandered through many unsettled places and sought instruction from many people, especially ascetic teachers; eventually, however, he turned to intense meditation or contemplation. After nearly ten years, he finally experienced "awakening" or "enlightenment" (*bodhi*) and then took up the life of an itinerant teacher—becoming widely known as "Shakyamuni" (sage of the Shakyas) or "*Tathágata*" (the one who went forth).

Are there still lessons for our lives today in these distant narratives and far-off experiences? Can we still appreciate the challenge—but also the hardship and distress—involved in the migrations between place and no-place, between settlement and unsettlement, and also the different senses or meanings of "desert" disclosed in them? The theologian Walter Brueggemann and two of his friends recently published a remarkable book titled *The Other Kingdom: Departing the Consumer Culture*. Pointing to the Exodus of the Israelites from Pharaoh's kingdom, the authors draw a parallel to our time, saying: "This departure into another kingdom [or mode of life] might be closer to the reality of our nature and what works best for our humanity. This *other* kingdom better speaks to the growing longing for an alternative culture, an alternative way of being together." The move from one life form to another is not smooth or painless but rather tough and challenging. The authors here speak of "departure" in the sense of farewell or parting of the ways (*Abschied*): "We use the word *departing* to remember and to re-perform the Israelites' Exodus into the wilderness away from Egypt, for the journey into a social order not based on [conspicuous] consumption seems equally imposing [today]." Elaborating more fully on the parallel, the authors present a vivid picture of the difficulties and hardships: "The analog in our time for being beyond Pharaoh's reach is being beyond the reach of financial credit systems, payday loan operators, developers, the bureaucracy, all the imperial institutions. The path into a neighborly culture can be considered a step into the wilderness, with its uncertainty and lack of visible means of support. The consumer culture, however, is so embedded in our habits and brain wiring that when we move toward the wilderness of covenant and mystery, we are always drawn back to a world of control and contract."[4]

The hardships and challenges of the turn-around are indeed formidable; in many ways they resemble the challenges presented by a move into monastic life or a monastic community. Political philosopher Alasdair MacIntyre famously concluded his book *After Virtue* with this line: "We are waiting not for a Godot, but for another—doubtless very different—St. Benedict." In a subsequent edition, he added this comment: "Benedict's greatness lay in making possible a quite new kind of institution, that of the monastery of prayer, learning and labor, in which and around which communities could not only survive, but flourish in a period of social and cultural darkness."[5] More recently, Italian philosopher Giorgio Agamben has drawn attention to the work of St. Francis and especially his foundation of the Franciscan order as an antidote or alternative to the world of law, property arrangements, and bureaucratic (including clerical) institutions. "What is perhaps the most precious legacy of Franciscanism," he writes, a legacy "to which the West must return ever anew," is "how to think a form-of-life, a human life entirely removed from the grasp of law, and a use of bodies and the world that would never be transformed into an appropriation." This means that Francis's legacy is "to think life as that which is never given as a property but only as a common use" (or common practice). By moving outside legal and contractual rules, St. Francis opened the path to a "poverty" not defined simply as a lack of property but as a path of redemption. Later Franciscan theorists, Agamben adds, insisted on the "separation of use/practice from ownership" and on the "genuine primordiality" of use/practice vis-à-vis rule or dominion.[6]

To be sure, the challenge of breaking loose from and transforming established conventions not only presents itself to monastic communities and spiritual leaders but also must be faced squarely by philosophy and human thinking as such. A prime example in this respect is the work of Martin Heidegger, the philosopher who famously renewed the "question of Being"—what it means for us to "be"—and whose writings are crucially placed under the aegis of a "turn-around" or *Kehre*. In articulating the needed turn-around, Heidegger appeals explicitly to Nietzsche's notion of the "growing desert," bringing this notion in connection with a profound "desertion" happening in our time: the desertion of and by Being, coupled with the pervasive oblivion of the question of Being (*Seinsverlassenheit/Seinsvergessenheit*). As he argues, this oblivion surrenders human life to the powers-that-be, the routines of settled ways of life anchored in self-satisfaction and the desire for appropriation (will to power)—that is, to devastation (*Verwüstung*). Turning away from established habits in his presentation is bound to be wrenching and painful. Curiously, Heidegger in this context uses Brueggemann's term "departure" in the sense of a courageous "farewell" (*Abschied*) from the routines of thoughtless everydayness. Basically, *Kehre* is meant to serve as a pathway or prelude to recovery in the direction of an "other beginning" (*anderer Anfang*). By the same token, *Kehre* is marked by a process of "expropriation" (*Enteignung*) whereby human beings are prevented from "appropriating" Being and exerting dominion over it. As Heidegger adds, such expropriation occurs under the emblem of the "nobility of poverty" (*Adel der Armut*) nurtured by genuine human care.[7]

In the present book, I have chosen as guides four spiritual leaders or pioneers whose writings have greatly influenced, and continue to influence, large numbers of people. I could have chosen a number of additional guides, as there is surely no shortage of influential mentors. I have selected the four figures discussed in this book—Paul Tillich, Raimon Panikkar, Thomas Merton, and Pope Francis—mainly because of their insistence on the need for radical *metanoia*, turnaround or *Kehre*. A main limitation of this choice is its central focus on Western exemplars of spiritual life. In part, this choice was motivated by the desire to keep the book within manageable limits. In addition, my selection was guided by the assumption or conviction that it is in Western societies where social and ecological spoliation or *Verwüstung* is most advanced and where turn-around is hence most urgently needed. Nevertheless, my cross-cultural and interfaith leanings or commitments have prompted me to add two further chapters extending my reflections on spirituality to other religious and spiritual traditions, especially to some of the vibrant traditions in the Islamic world and also in India and East Asia. I still can be accused of neglecting some of the rich folk traditions of spirituality found in Africa, Latin America, and the Oceanic world. But I leave this exploration to others more competent and more thoroughly steeped in these legacies.[8]

The four guides chosen for this book are to a large extent bridge-builders or champions of a "holistic" recovery from modern fragmentation. The bridges they build seek to reconnect the transtemporal and the temporal, the "sacred" and the "secular," and also theoretical insight and social praxis. In academic terms, their endeavors link together—in fruitful tension—theology with philosophy, Christian dogmatics with the humanities and social sciences. An outstanding exemplar of such intellectual breadth is the "dialectical" theology and spirituality of Paul Tillich. Chapter 1, devoted to him, guides the reader through the different stages of his intellectual and theological development. During his early phase, prior to his emigration to America, Tillich was embroiled in the political turmoil of the Weimar Republic, which pitted against each other bourgeois capitalism, collectivist communism, and racial nativism (fascism)—movements that, for him, were the result of radical egocentrism or mundane anthropocentrism. As an antidote or counterfoil he formulated the idea of a "religious socialism" that would reconnect prophetic expectations and concrete historical possibilities as well as individual freedom and social solidarity. During the same period, Tillich also coined the conceptual triad of external "heteronomy," self-centered "autonomy," and "theonomy," with the last term dialectically overcoming and sublating the other categories. His book *The Socialist Decision* offered a stunning theological-political analysis of the forces active in the Weimar Republic, predicting (correctly) that the choice would ultimately come down to that between religious socialism and fascist "barbarism."

Following his emigration to America, Tillich devoted his energies mainly to the formulation of his "dialectical theology," although he never abandoned his concern with political (or political-theological) issues. In his treatment, dialectical theology meant basically an effort to overcome the radical separation of the "sacred" and the "profane" (a dichotomy championed for some time by Karl Barth) in the direction of a mutual correlation and contestation. "Correlation" here means that the sacred or divine confronts the secular-profane world with a prophetic challenge or demand, while secularity anchored in concrete experience prevents religion from evaporating into wishful thinking or pious platitudes. As one should note, Tillich's "dialectics" is indebted to Hegel's philosophy while eschewing the latter's idealist teleology. The strongest influence on Tillich, however, came from Friedrich Schelling, who, in a way, had concretized Hegel by elaborating a dialectical relation between "existence" and "essence" or between life and spirit. The major achievement of Tillich's later years was the completion of his *Systematic Theology*, a work in which dialectical spirituality in the sense of a tensional world-God relationship reaches its most eloquent expression. A major guidepost in this work is the theme of the promised coming of the "Kingdom of God," a coming that for Tillich has both an "inner-historical" and a "transhistorical" character, thus holding immanence and transcendence in delicate balance. While fervently pleading for openness to the divine promise (and linking its immanent aspect again with religious socialism), he became increasingly fearful that—without serious *metanoia*—the ongoing process of militarization and spoliation would lead to a new barbarism that would take the form of global war and nuclear holocaust.

In the case of Raimon Panikkar, Tillich's dialectical approach is transformed into an emphatic—though tensional or differentiated—"holism." The key expressions Panikkar uses to pinpoint his holistic faith are "sacred secularity" and "cosmotheandric vision," a vision that links closely together the dimensions of the divine, the human, and the natural-material world. The notion of "sacred secularity" surfaces in some of his early writings dealing with religious worship in secular modernity. Detecting in our time a special "*kairos*" or "axial" possibility, he argues that "only worship can prevent secularization from becoming inhuman, and only secularization can save worship from being meaningless."[9] The upshot is that, in the new dispensation, the secular or temporal surfaces also as "sacred"—though not without engendering mutual rifts, contestations, and possible derailments. In subsequent writings, Panikkar extended his holistic outlook to the interreligious and cross-cultural domain. In this respect, he emerged as one of the leading thinkers of religious and cultural pluralism, a perspective that—radically opposed to both cultural absolutism and relativism—relies on the forging of lateral ties between cultures through dialogue and mutual interaction. One of Panikkar's persistent targets of criticism in this context is "globalism," understood as the policy of cultural-political hegemony or imperialism. His book *Cultural Disarmament* formulates a "philosophy of peace" that, in opposition to *pax Romana* or *pax Americana*, urges the cultivation of mutual recognition and nonviolent cross-cultural engagement. The concluding part of the chapter devoted to Panikkar explores the compatibility of religious holism with radical prophetic demands. As I try to show, Panikkar's holism—properly construed as operating on the deep level of "ontological trust"—does not exclude or cancel his endorsement of the prophetic demand for justice in the world.

In one of his writings titled *Blessed Simplicity*, Panikkar presented "monkhood" or monastic life not as a special occupation or profession but rather as a disposition constitutive of humanity as such: the disposition to care about existence and the point of "being" (and thus to overcome the oblivion of Being, *Seinsvergessenheit*). This is precisely the meaning that we find in Thomas Merton's turn to monastic life. To this extent, Merton's stay at Gethsemani abbey should be seen not as an aberrant exception but as an exemplary model of a thoughtful human life well lived. Under the rubric of "pathways to solitude," the chapter of my book devoted to Merton explores first of all his lifelong commitment to meditation and depth reflection as an antidote to absorption into the mindless busyness of the contemporary world. As he writes at one point: "Contemplation is the highest expression of man's intellectual and spiritual life. It is that life itself, fully aware. What contemplation also discovers, however, is that life is not self-generated, but proceeds from a source which is hidden and discloses itself basically in a call or provocation."[10] One aspect that is crucial in Merton's account is that meditation or contemplation is not simply a form of introspection or retreat into inner selfhood. His texts are emphatic in rejecting the linkage between contemplation and the Cartesian *cogito ergo sum*; this means that going inside, for him, is always also a going-forward to others (and to God). Thus, contemplative solitude is closely connected with solidarity or communion. In his pithy formulation: "Go into the desert (of solitude) not to escape other human beings but in order to find them (in God)."[11]

The chapter turns at this point to Merton's lifelong endeavor to chart a course connecting or reconciling monastic life with active world engagement and social solidarity. The texts reviewed for this purpose are mainly *Contemplation in a World of Action*, *Conjectures of a Guilty Bystander*, and *Cold War Letters* (texts revealing a steady crescendo of social commitment). The writings clearly refute the stereotype of Merton as a world-denying recluse "heading for the woods." At the same time, they testify to his courageous effort to keep his head above the cauldron of prevailing ideological slogans, media indoctrination, and political mind control. What the texts demonstrate most forcefully, however, is Merton's faithfulness to the prophetic call for justice and peace, which cannot be relegated to "another world" but has to be shouldered (prayerfully) in our time. His denunciation of such evils as racism, imperialism, warmongering, reckless profiteering, and senseless consumerism is among the most vivid and engaging social protests in the spiritual literature. The conclusion of the chapter takes up Merton's ecumenical endeavors and his growing fascination during his last decade with Asian spirituality. Most memorable in this connection are his writings on the Mahatma Gandhi, on Buddhism, and on Taoism—writings that clearly reveal

his ability to move beyond the "one-eyed giant" of Western ratio-
nalism and (presumed) cultural supremacy as well as his openness to
worldwide spiritual resources. In this sense, Merton fully validated
the notion of contemplation and spiritual mindfulness as the gateway
to the depth dimension of our shared humanity.

In our present time, some of the spiritual impulses motivating
Merton are continued and reinvigorated in the apostolic work of
Pope Francis, who himself chose his name in honor and in memory of St. Francis and the Franciscan monastic tradition. Chapter 4,
titled "Herald of Glad Tidings," shows how the pope's teachings and
writings can serve as a bulwark against global chaos and the growing wasteland or desert of our world. The chapter starts by recalling
some of the pontiff's statements at the war memorial in Redipuglia,
Italy, where he denounced war as "utter madness" and also pointed
to some of the underlying causes of devastation: "Greed, intolerance,
the lust for power ... these motives underlie the decision to go to
war." These motives, he added, powerfully persist in our present
time, unleashing new wars "fought piecemeal, with crimes, massacre,
wanton destruction."[12] In some of his writings and speeches of recent
years, Francis strongly attacked a whole host of the ills and "diseases"
in today's world: the growing intolerance between countries, races,
and creeds; the massive political and economic inequality between
rich and poor, powerful and powerless; the rise of a new idolatry of
the "God of money"; the spreading "culture" of consumption and
waste; and above all the glorification of violence, turning the whole
world into a battlefield. In the face of this battery of derailments,
miseries, and dangers, the pontiff urges people to step back from the
brink of the abyss and undergo a radical turning or "*metanoia.*" Only
such a turning, he stresses, can lead our desert world to social and
spiritual renewal—which is a precondition of the proclamation of
"glad tidings," of the promise of God's kingdom.

As indicated earlier, the concluding two chapters of this book venture beyond the confines of Western religion, especially the confines of
traditional Christian spirituality. The aim of both chapters is twofold:
to lend greater historical depth to the preceding discussions focused
on the recent and contemporary period and to add a broader cross-
cultural and interfaith dimension to the book as a whole. Chapter 5

offers a comparative exploration of different modes of spirituality as found in Christian and Islamic traditions. At this point I introduce a distinction between chiefly two kinds of spirituality (a distinction that had been present but not explicitly thematized in prior chapters): namely, between a basically vertical and a basically lateral orientation, that is, between an orientation aiming at ultimate fusion or union with God's transcendence and one reaching out to other human beings in love (*agape*) and practical service. While admiring the "transcendentalist" fervor of the first type, the chapter alerts readers to possible destructive or violent repercussions for worldly, interhuman relations (repercussions following the motto "*fiat iustitia pereat mundus*"). Although acknowledging possible manipulative dangers, the chapter (and the book as a whole) pleads in favor of the *agape*- and service-oriented type of spirituality. The concluding chapter 6 explores prominent Christian "encounters" with Asian spirituality, with a focus on Buddhism and especially on the Buddhist notions of "emptiness" (*sunyata*) and "compassion" (*karuna*). For purposes of illustration, the chapter returns to three of the spiritual guides discussed in earlier chapters: Tillich, Panikkar, and Merton. As it happens, all three in their later years developed an intensive interest in Zen Buddhism, though from different backgrounds and with different focal concerns.

The epilogue turns to a famous sermon by the German mystic Meister Eckhart: "*Beati pauperes spiritu*," "Blessed are the poor in spirit." What emerges in that sermon is a fascinating emphasis on radical self-emptying and nonpossession—an emphasis that is not very far removed from the Buddhist notion of "emptiness" (*sunyata*). Only the experience and confession of such dispossession can lead from desert to renewal, from poverty onto the path of spiritual redemption.

Chapter One

Faithful Expectation

Hommage à Paul Tillich

In which of these groups do you belong—among those who respond to the prophetic spirit, or among those who close their ears and hearts to it?

—Paul Tillich, *The Shaking of the Foundations*

Half a century ago, in 1965, Paul Tillich passed away. At that time, he was by all counts the leading and most highly esteemed Protestant theologian in America. In the meantime, many things have happened—among them the Cold War, the dismantling of the Soviet Union, and finally the rise of ISIS. In the course of these events, Tillich's legacy more and more faded from view. It is true that today there are efforts to revitalize that legacy and to foreground the "radical" and forward-pointing elements of his work. However, with some notable exceptions, the effort is undertaken mainly by professional theologians with the aim of "radicalizing" his *theological* teachings.[1] What tends to be forgotten is that, for Tillich, religious faith was always closely entwined with culture and social conditions, which means that, apart from being a theologian, he was also a public intellectual trying to take the "pulse of his age." It is this linkage of faith and social reality that, in my view, is at the heart of Tillich's work. If this is correct (as I believe), revitalizing his work cannot be left solely to theologians and experts in religious studies but must be shouldered also by humanists and social scientists, including political philosophers. In fact, I want to claim that his continued relevance depends on that collaboration.

Viewed from this perspective, Tillich's work in large measure emerges as "untimely" or "out of season"; it is situated at a steep angle to modern society and modern Western culture (what Heidegger called modern "metaphysics"). This does not mean that he was an "outsider" or that his thought arose out of "nowhere" (he was clearly rooted in the Christian tradition). Rather, his entire work can be seen as the result of an intense critical struggle with some dominant thought patterns or worldviews of modernity. Without such engagement and struggle, all high-sounding words—like "God" or "perennial ideas"—were for him *flatus vocis* (empty sounds) devoid of grounding in human experience. At the same time, while always exploring experiential warrants, Tillich was unwilling to surrender himself to "worldliness" or the changing fashions of the day. In this respect, his outlook resonated in many ways with the *Dialectic of Enlightenment*, penned by Max Horkheimer and Theodor Adorno (his one-time colleagues in Frankfurt). In the following I examine some of the "untimely" (and to this extent "radical") features of Tillich's work, considered as the product of a public intellectual cum theologian. Three aspects are highlighted: his defense of "religious socialism," his "dialectical" political theology, and his portrayal of both the promises and the dangers of the emerging global culture.

"Religious Socialism"

One of the more astonishing aspects of Tillich's revitalization today is the relatively scant attention being paid to his "socialist" roots and commitments. No doubt this fact has something to do with the taboo character of the term "socialism" in America. Still, one may wonder about the extent of the theologians' accommodation on this issue. It is true that, during his time in America (especially the postwar "red scare" period), Tillich himself considerably toned down and even avoided direct references to socialism or socialist agendas. However, he never directly recanted or repudiated his socialist texts (written mostly before his emigration). In fact, one can say that, until the very end of his life, there was a strong current or undercurrent of socialist sensibilities—and this was quite in keeping with his view of the healing and bonding character of religion. To be sure, one has to note the distinctive meaning of "socialism" for Tillich. It surely had nothing in common with the materialistic collectivism that, under the label of "communism," had emerged in the Soviet Union. To mark the difference, Tillich preferred the phrase "religious socialism." But even here, caution is required. The phrase did not imply a social system guided by or operating under the tutelage of an established Church—an arrangement that would have violated a basic cornerstone of modern democracy: the separation (or, better, differentiation) of church and state.[2]

Tillich's socialist leanings emerged first in the heady months after World War I when Germany was in the throes of radical change. The German emperor abdicated in December 1918, and the Protestant (evangelical) church—a main pillar of the Empire—was in disarray. A dissident church movement (calling itself the "New Church Alliance") arose at that time, and Tillich was immediately attracted to it. The movement issued a programmatic statement, signed by Tillich, that charted a clear pathway to the future. Among the main positions advocated in the statement were these: support for the emerging "republican" or democratic regime infused by a "farsighted socialism" in which the "personal worth" of each member would be upheld over against the "capitalist egotism" of the Bismarck period, alignment with the international peace movement in opposition to nationalism and militarism, and, finally, construction of an international league to replace the old system of brute power politics. Tillich did not remain for long in that movement but continued to present lectures in the same dissident spirit—much to the dismay of old-style Protestants desiring to regain their "established" status. Distilling the gist of these speeches, Tillich (joined by a friend) in mid-1919 issued a report under the title "Socialism as a Question of the Church." The report (I rely on Ronald Stone's summary) insisted that Christian faith is not purely transcendental or otherworldly; nor does it counsel a purely personal or inward retreat. Rather, in accord with gospel teachings, it necessarily has a social impact and relevance: its spirit favors some social arrangements over others. Specifically, Christianity bears a closer affinity with socialism than with capitalism (at least in its monopolistic form). This affinity is demonstrated by the tendency of industrial capitalism to support militarism and war, in opposition to Christian teachings and practices.[3]

A year later, in 1920, Tillich joined a new group in Berlin that proved to be even more congenial to his religious commitment: the "*Kairos* Circle," which he served as a leader for four years. Bringing together a number of socially engaged intellectuals from several academic disciplines, the circle was mainly concerned with such issues as the relation of faith and society, the connection between the eternal and the temporal or historical, and the nature and goal of socialist society. The crucial topic, of course, was pinpointed by the term "*kairos*" (meaning "right time" or fulfilled time): How can the eternal or divine penetrate into the temporal? How can the sacred manifest itself in the secular or social? As Tillich stated in a lead essay in 1922, the term implies a call or a demand issued to temporality or history from the "depth of the Unconditional"—where the latter reflects an absolute or "ultimate concern." Issuing from a level transcending all particular time, such a call is contained in the biblical *Shemah Israel*: "Thou shalt love the Lord your God with *all* your heart, *all* your mind, and *all* your being"—to which is added the coequal demand to "love your neighbor as yourself." Only where these two demands (which are one) are fully heard and followed can one speak of the possibility of a *kairos*. For Tillich, the period after World War I bore the mark of a possible *kairos* in the form of "religious socialism," which brings together the love of God and the love of fellow beings in the world. To be sure, in kairological terms, the absolute or "Unconditional" can never be fully temporalized or fulfilled *in* history but remains a prophetic demand. To this extent, the ultimate "Kingdom of God" is not simply a historical event.[4]

Tillich further explored this kairological theme a year later in a major essay titled "Basic Principles of Religious Socialism." The essay delves immediately into the difficult relation of the two poles: the sacred (vertical) and the temporal (horizontal). In the analysis of a given social situation, Tillich remarks, two basic perspectives can be distinguished: the "sacramental attitude" that shuns history and the "rationalist" or "historically critical attitude." The first outlook clings resolutely to "the presence of the divine"; the second seeks to analyze what is happening from a purely human and "critical rational" vantage point. In contrast to both of these outlooks, religious socialism in Tillich's account adopts a "prophetic attitude" that finds the unity of the sacred and the temporal in their tensional relation: "Prophetism grasps the coming of what *should be* from its living connection with the present that is given" (that is, the potential in its connection with the actual).[5] For religious socialism, he adds, the prophetic outlook is "essential." For it must recognize that "the presence of the Unconditional is the *prius* of all conditioned social action" or that "unconditioned meaning is the *prius* to *all* forms of meaning." Here the kairological aspect emerges. "We have used the word *Kairos*," Tillich states, "for the content of the prophetic view of history. It signifies a moment of time filled with unconditioned meaning and demand." As he explains: *kairos* does not contain a "prediction" of the future; nor does it signify a merely abstract demand or postulated "ideal." Rather, it denotes "the fulfilled moment of time in which the present and the future, the holy that is given and the holy that is demanded meet, and from whose concrete tension the new creation proceeds."[6]

In the remainder of the essay, the goal or *telos* of religious socialism is more fully elaborated. In this context, Tillich introduces a terminology that has become a trademark of this thought: the triadic distinction between "autonomy," "heteronomy," and "theonomy." Like most modern thinkers, the theologian appreciates human "autonomy" when it is seen as a bulwark against all forms of political, cultural, and clerical domination, that is, against oppressive "heteronomy." Taken in this sense, autonomy refers to the creative, liberating élan captured in Kant's "*sapere aude!*" However, when self-centered and pursued without limits, this élan can also take on destructive features—which Tillich describes as "demonic." Unleashed in the political domain, the demonic potential takes the form of a "this-worldly utopianism" exemplified by chauvinistic nationalism (fascism) and Stalinist communism. In opposition to these derailments, some people glorify submission to heteronomy, sometimes backed up by divine authority. This glorification can also foster "demonic" aberrations, especially an "otherworldly utopianism" exemplified by "theocratic movements" in which the "absolute rule of God" or the "sovereignty of the Unconditional" is directly imposed on society. In contrast to these dystopias, "theonomy" for Tillich seeks to correlate the sacred and the temporal and, to this extent, preserves the "prophetic" outlook on history. Wedded to this correlation, religious socialism necessarily maintains an ambivalent, "dialectical" relation to society: it contains within itself a prophetic "No" to the actual situation, but also a "Yes" to the potential. It takes its stand against both otherworldly and this-worldly "demonries."[7]

To be sure, religious socialism for Tillich was not a fixed doctrine or party platform but rather a tentative formula open to revisions and corrections. As it happened, the growing fragility of the Weimar Republic prompted him to accept the need for a more robust political engagement. In 1929 he joined the Social Democratic Party and endorsed some of its "realistic" policies.[8] To some extent, one can surmise, his outlook was also influenced by his 1929 move to Frankfurt, where, as a professor at the university (succeeding Max Scheler), he came in close contact with the Institute for Social Research, most of whose members shared left-Hegelian or "humanist Marxist" leanings. According to Ronald Stone, Tillich at that time became even "more directly involved in active socialist politics than most Frankfurt theorists."[9] The intellectual high point of his engagement, however, came in early 1933 with the publication of *The Socialist Decision*—shortly before the Nazi takeover, which triggered his dismissal and emigration.

By all counts, *The Socialist Decision* is one of Tillich's major mature works—a chef d'oeuvre of both political theology and political philosophy. As he makes clear in his "Foreword," the book seeks to profile and concretize further the meaning of "religious socialism" used in his earlier writings. This effort was needed in view of the perilous condition of Europe and Germany at the time: the rise of extremist political movements on the Right and the Left, accompanied by violent clashes. In the face of these perils, Tillich stated, it was only "by a common socialist decision that the fate of death now hanging over the peoples of Europe can be averted." Hence, a strong commitment to socialism (of some kind) was imperative. The issue, of course, was the character of this commitment. For Tillich, socialism could not be identified with "scientism," or the belief in necessary social progress; nor could Marxism be equated with Stalinist communism. *The Socialist Decision* aimed to correct prevalent misconstruals: "It holds fast to Marxism and defends it against the pure activism of a younger generation; but it also rejects the scientism and dogmatic materialism of an older generation." More precisely, this means that the text harkens back to the "real Marx" (that is, the "humanist" Marx) and a concept of dialectic in which "necessity and freedom are conjoined." Regarding the "religious" element, Tillich's stance coincides with a "moderately prophetic" outlook (shunning all dogmatism or orthodoxy). "Socialism," the foreword concludes, "has to be sober in its analysis, and sober in the attitude of 'expectation' it assumes. . . . [It] requires the clearest, most sober realism—though it must be a 'faithful realism' (*gläubiger Realismus*), a realism of expectation."[10]

In its opening section, the text lays the groundwork of the study by sketching the outlines of a philosophical anthropology largely derived from "existentialist" teachings. As Tillich states firmly: "The roots of political thought must be sought in human being itself"—but this human being is internally split or in tension, namely, between its past (*whence*) and its future (*whither*). Tillich calls the former "origin" or "natural being" and the second "freedom" and "consciousness." Genuine political thinking, he elaborates, must proceed on this tensional basis and find its roots "simultaneously in 'being' and consciousness" (a dual anchorage captured in Heidegger's depiction of human *Dasein* as a "thrown project"). Differently put, one must recognize that human life "proceeds in a tension between [thrown] dependence on the origin and [projected] independence." From a political angle, it is important to note that the natural roots of existence (*whence*) has itself a dual status: it can be salutary and enabling or confining and repressing. In the latter case, natural being gives rise to the "myth of origin," which—according to Tillich—is "the root of all conservative and Romantic thought in politics." In opposition to a nostalgic "return to the womb," consciousness confronts human existence with an "unconditional demand": the demand to shape its own future (*whither*) freely and without dependence. This rupture with the past is "the root of liberal, democratic, and socialist thought in politics," that is, the root of (Western) modernity. However, cut loose from all dependence, liberal modernity also shatters the mutual dependence between human beings as well as the interdependence of humanity and nature, leading to intense strife on all levels. Hence, a new stage has to be found—the stage of "socialism"—in which the enabling potency of the origin can be enlisted for a renewed "just" interdependence: "Justice is the 'true' power of being; in it the (enabling) intention of the origin is fulfilled."[11]

As indicated in its opening pages, the aim of the study is to develop a (political) philosophy of history coupled with hints of soteriology. In the present context, only the main lines of the argument can briefly be traced. As mentioned before, "political Romanticism" for Tillich signals a return to the past through the erection of a static "myth of origin" in which the repressive aspect of the origin comes to cancel its enabling side. The first break with the myth occurred in Judaism, especially in the prophetic tradition, where "time was elevated above space" through the forecast of a "new heaven and new earth." As Tillich notes, however, the break was not complete, because the prophetic message and historical Judaism cannot be equated. In fact, there has always been a struggle between Old Testament prophetism and the persistent lure of the "origin" in the form of Jewish nationalism.[12] The second break with myth occurred in the European Enlightenment, which liberated "autonomous consciousness" by suppressing the dimension of the origin (and even the "depth dimension of existence" altogether). At this point, particular things or objects in their finitude became the chief targets of scientific "knowledge and manipulation." Before proceeding, Tillich distinguishes between two types of political Romanticism: a "reactionary" (or conservative) type and a "revolutionary" (or populist) type. The first type appeals mainly to older elites, like nobles, landowners, and high clergy, while the second caters to people alienated from bourgeois modernity and seeking relief in myths and rituals. The second type—against which Tillich's book is basically directed—is "revolutionary" only in the sense of fashioning a new mythology (like the Nazi myth of the "Third Reich") while canceling or suppressing all elements of modern autonomy or emancipation.[13]

The ensuing chapters of *The Socialist Decision* deal, respectively, with Western modernity, the rise of bourgeois society with its intrinsic antinomies, and the prospect of a socialist overcoming or "sublation" of antinomies. As Tillich observes, in Western modernity the myth of origin was shattered by the two prongs of Protestantism and Enlightenment: the first discarding medieval religious bonds, the second removing political and intellectual forms of heteronomy. Launched by these two prongs, modern bourgeois society ushered in the sway of "autonomous this-worldliness." Emerging from the "dissolution" of all prior conditions, bourgeois society involves the triumph of a human-centered project that "subjugates an objectified world to its own purposes." In its optimistic self-understanding, modern "liberal" society claims to guarantee social equilibrium and harmony—a claim that is spurious. For, by subjugating the "objectified world," this society creates an antinomy between humanity and nature and, in its linkage with capitalism, a class division between rich and poor. Moreover, antagonisms of this kind spill over from domestic society into the international arena, leading to colonial struggles between the West and non-West, between center and periphery. All these diremptions cry out for resolution—which cannot be found in the confines of bourgeois modernity. What socialism brings is a radical change of paradigm, a leap from the actual condition to the reign of potentiality. In doing so, socialism recaptures the "enabling" spirit of the "origin" with its promise of just relationships. To this extent, its aim is not merely to overcome class division and exploitation but rather to end dehumanization and the reification of the world in all its dimensions.[14]

What even this brief summary should convey is the bold analytical grasp and also the continued relevance of Tillich's study. Although penned during the Weimar Republic's plunge into collapse, its analytical categories have lost little of their cogency and disturbing quality. To some extent—one might say—the cultural and political afflictions of Weimar are haunting the contemporary world on a global scale. There is still the lure of "political Romanticism" both in the form of old-style cultural and religious elitism and in the more radical guise of nationalistic (and quasi-fascist) populism. And there is the massive presence of globalized financial capitalism with its offshoots of domestic division between rich and poor (the 1 percent and the 99 percent) and the worldwide contrast between North and South, between center and periphery. Finally, there are rumblings, here and there, of a paradigm shift heralding transformation and a better future. On all these levels, Tillich's text was uncannily farsighted. It also was pioneering on a strictly philosophical level: in many ways, his look anticipated by a decade Horkheimer and Adorno's *Dialectic of Enlightenment* (composed in 1943). Like that work, *The Socialist Decision* was "dialectical" in character—in the sense not of a logically grounded Hegelian teleology but of Adorno's "negative dialectics," in which the future is a sheltered expectation.[15] There was one further sign of farsightedness in *The Socialist Decision*. Toward the end, Tillich writes this lapidary sentence: "The salvation of European society from a return to barbarism lies in the hands of socialism."[16] As it happened, this return to barbarism was just around the corner.

Dialectical Theology

Despite initial hesitations, Tillich emigrated in 1933 from Germany to New York, where he joined the Union Theological Seminary. With this move he entered the "New World"—a world that was also in many ways new and alien to him. Clearly, despite some cultural overlaps, U.S. America at the time was not Weimar Germany, where his formative experiences were rooted. For one thing, the political and ideological spectrum in America was more uniform or narrow than in Weimar. Basically, the American regime was shaped by British-style "liberalism," which had initially emerged in opposition to old-style Tory conservatism. In the course of America's development, the older Tory elements—to the extent they survived—had blended steadily into the dominant liberal-bourgeois structure (adding only occasional cultural reservations). Thus America left little or no room for the "reactionary Romanticism" Tillich had described. On the other hand, Tillich's "populist Romanticism" was at best an undercurrent (held in abeyance for the time being). What occupied center stage in America was the "bourgeois-liberal" principle in its alliance with industrial and financial capitalism. From the vantage point of this dominant ideology, the chief political and economic enemy was—more than fascism—the current of socialism and communism (often with little effort to distinguish the various branches). Given this ideological situation, Tillich, as a prominent "socialist emigré," faced a quandary or dilemma. The quandary was intensified by the fact that Tillich himself regarded socialism not as an abstract ideal but as a concrete movement growing out of real-life experiences and needs. However, in the absence of a viable workers' movement, how was it possible to make a "socialist decision"?[17]

Viewed from this angle, Tillich's so-called retreat from politics into theology in America—an aspect sometimes praised, sometimes bemoaned—gains at least some plausibility and intelligibility. Clearly, his initial condition in the country was delicate as a resident alien (he did not become a citizen until 1940). Moreover, as he frequently stated, he came to America not only to preach but also to learn and absorb what is valuable. Most important, the period after 1933 proved to be very challenging for him precisely as a theologian. The situation of Christian churches in Germany at that time was extremely precarious—a condition he observed attentively and anxiously. There was a concerted effort on the part of the Nazi regime to co-opt Christian, especially Protestant, churches—an effort that was to some extent deplorably successful (especially among so-called German Christians). As a theologian who had always stressed the linkage of religion and social life, Tillich was compelled to profile his position more clearly. The Swiss theologian Karl Barth had made a sharp cut between religion and the "world," between the sacred and the profane—a cut that tended to exile churches to a "holy mountain" while leaving the secular realm stranded. Given his longstanding "kairological" leanings, Tillich could not accept this dichotomy, which, in effect, weakened or undercut the "prophetic" quality of faith. As he came to see, the German situation exemplified the need for a more adequate "dialectical" theology, that is, a theology that resists both the "politicization" (or political co-optation) of religion and its "privatization" in the inner lives of believers.[18]

As one should note, the term "dialectical" here has a special meaning. Basically, the term denotes not a purely logical formula but rather the emblem of a concrete struggle and experiential engagement.

For Tillich, the Barthian dichotomy of sacred and profane could not be resolved through a simple fusion or amalgamation. Rather, the two categories or dimensions had to be recognized as distinct—but distinct precisely in their correlation and mutual contestation. In this view, the sacred or divine confronts everything profane or secular with a prophetic judgment; in turn, the secular prevents the divine from evaporating into abstract idealism or wishful thinking. As previously indicated, Tillich's "dialectics" stands on the shoulders of Hegel's philosophy—minus the latter's idealist teleology or eschatology. The same relation obtains to Marx's work—where "orthodox" historical determinism gives way to "humanist" praxis. As also indicated, Tillich's argument resembles in some ways Adorno's "negative dialectics"—not consciously but by way of serendipity. One major influence that needs to be mentioned (and one that he always acknowledged) is the work of Friedrich Schelling, who, in a way, had concretized Hegel by elaborating a dialectic between "existence" and "essence," actuality and potentiality, or between life and spirit. Significant impulses also derive from Schelling's theory of the "world ages," from his distinction between enabling and repressive "origin" (or nature), and from his notion of sequentially correlated "potencies." As Tillich observes at one point: "Only Schelling . . . recognized that reality is not only the manifestation of pure essence (spirit) but also of its contradiction and, above all, that human existence itself is an expression of the contradiction of essence."[19]

Needless to say, dialectics in Tillich's sense was not always easy to maintain in the American context because of the close interpenetration of culture and religion. Despite the official separation of church and state, religion over the years had been tightly co-opted by popular culture and the "American way of life"—so tightly as to render a prophetic judgment of culture nearly impossible. Christianity in particular has been the target of massive co-optation, to the point that some writers have been able to portray Jesus as a "national icon" and American Christian faith as part of the "marketplace of culture."[20] Religion, however, not only pervades the domestic market in America but also spills over into foreign policy and global agendas. Social theorist Tzvetan Todorov speaks correctly in this context about the proclivity of American culture to promote global "millenarianism" or "messianism"—a proclivity that, in some quarters, boils over into a hankering for Armageddon or the "end time" of history. When this happens, religion turns into a weapon of violence and global domination; in Tillich's vocabulary, faith decays from an enabling and salvific potency into a "demonic" force of destruction. In the words of Richard Niebuhr (another major theologian): "When closely allied with emperors and governors, merchants and entrepreneurs," and living "at peace in culture," faith "loses its force, corruption enters with idolatry, and the church . . . suffers corruption in turn."[21]

Throughout his three decades in America, Tillich remained close to the sentiments expressed by Niebuhr and, to this extent, remained faithful to theological "dialectics." During the 1930s he repeatedly visited Europe, trying to alert people in numerous talks to the terrible dangers of "populist Romanticism" (that is, fascism) while also holding up the vision of a better future. A noticeable undercurrent in his speeches was the idea of "religious socialism," though often couched in new vocabulary. In 1937 he presented a lecture at an ecumenical conference in Oxford on the theme "The Kingdom of God and History." In this lecture the notion of the "Kingdom" was clearly a prophetic symbol and an antidote to the derailments of the time. For Tillich, the notion is lodged at the cusp of immanence and transcendence, of history and transhistory—which is the proper locus of a dialectical theology. Seen from this angle, history as such is not meaningful but receives its meaning from a deeper potentiality. Differently and more theologically put: world history is not itself salvific, but salvation is the meaning and promise of world history. In Tillich's words: "The Kingdom of God is a symbolic expression of the ultimate meaning of existence. The social and political character of this symbol indicates a special relation between the ultimate meaning of existence and the ultimate meaning of human history." Apart from disclosing an ultimate horizon, the Kingdom also embodies a prophetic judgment of the derailments or "demonic" forces operating in history, in particular the forces of (fascist) nationalism, monopolistic capitalism, and collectivist Bolshevism. In trying to find a concrete historical agency carrying forward the transhistorical *telos*, Tillich invoked again the idea of "religious socialism," seen now as an immanent warrant of a divinely transcendent purpose.[22]

Tillich spelled out some of the more strategic implications of religiously socialist leanings roughly at the same time in an essay dealing with Christian churches and Marxism. As he pointed out, churches were, on the whole, quite ignorant of Marxist teachings; a first step therefore should be an effort to acquaint oneself with and "acquire an exact knowledge" of these teachings. Once this is done, it becomes possible to discern the ambivalent character of Marxism, that is, to distinguish the "enabling" and forward-looking aspects from the more sinister and "demonic" features. The latter features were obvious in Stalinist Bolshevism—and were almost exclusively stressed in public discussion. On the enabling side, however, a different picture emerges: Tillich believed that Christians actually could find allies in Marxists critical of fascist nationalism and exploitative capitalism. Viewed from this perspective, Marxism emerges as a "secularized and politicized form of Christian propheticism." To be sure, a caveat needs to be observed: Christian propheticism can never be simply collapsed into an immanent movement, whether Marxist or communist or Christian socialist: "The practical strategy of the Church as a whole is a continuous attempt to make herself a representation and *anticipation* of the Kingdom of God and its righteousness." Yet churches cannot simply abscond: they have to testify and give witness to the *promise* of the Kingdom here and now. To this extent, their task is to find the right (dialectical) balance between "religious reservation from history and religious obligation toward history."[23]

Such a balanced posture became particularly urgent with the onset of World War II in 1939. Throughout the war years, Tillich engaged himself actively on the side of the allied powers, given that their struggle was chiefly aimed at the defeat of fascism. As is well known, the theologian beamed a large number of radio messages across the ocean to Germany in the hope of weakening the Nazi regime.[24] However, one should also note certain distinctive accents in his perception of "war aims." Above all, in Tillich's view, the war was strictly a struggle against fascism—not a prelude to a global campaign against communism (represented at the time by the Soviet Union). Faithful to his Christian-socialist commitments, he hoped that the outcome of the war would lead to a cleansing of dominant ideologies in both the

West and the East, in the sense that capitalism would be cured of its monopolistic tendencies and Russian communism of its collectivist and antihumanist traits.[25] In the midst of his concrete engagements, to be sure, Tillich never forgot about necessary prophetic correctives in political life. A major articulation of propheticism can be found in his formulation of a set of "Protestant Principles" in 1942—a formulation that is dialectical through and through. Its starting point is that Protestantism affirms "the absolute majesty of God alone" and rejects any co-optation of the divine by worldly powers. At the same time, the statement opposes the expulsion of the divine from the world and hence the rigid "separation of a sacred from a secular realm." All in all, while not endorsing any simple fusion or blending, Protestantism maintains the (dialectical) linkage of religion and culture and thus calls into question the dichotomy of "religious transcendence and cultural immanence."[26]

The end of World War II brought the defeat of Nazi Germany, which Tillich had actively promoted. But the aftermath also brought a stalemate between the superpowers and thus ushered in the prolongation of the conflict between liberal capitalism and communism that Tillich had feared. This prolongation was disappointing for him on many levels, especially with regard to his hopes for European and German reconstruction. As chairman of the Council for a Democratic Germany (established in 1944), Tillich argued for global détente, more specifically for cooperation between the West and Russia, as a necessary precondition for European revival and the rebuilding of Germany as a whole. The harsh realities of the ensuing Cold War put an end to these hopes.[27] In the midst of the immense tribulations of the period, Tillich found the time to write a thoughtful general assessment of the prevailing historical constellation under the title "The World Situation." In its social and political analysis, the text in many ways was an updated version of *The Socialist Decision*. Despite the resounding defeat of German fascism, the world for Tillich was still in the throes of the familiar constellation of social forces and ideological doctrines, especially the clash between bourgeois-capitalist structures and various socialist or communist counterforces. As he wrote: The present world situation is "the outcome of the rise, the triumph, and the crisis of what we may term 'bourgeois society.'" The development of that society occurred over several centuries and through a number of revolutions. Yet, precisely in its triumph or victory, bourgeois society has revealed its dialectical "underside," that is, the "disintegration" of social life exemplified by class struggle, ethnic struggles, and other conflicts all over the world.[28]

Although living at the time in the heartland of "bourgeois society," Tillich was not reticent in his critique. In his view, there had been a breakdown of the foundation of that society, namely, "the conviction of automatic harmony between individual interest and the general interest." What had become obvious was that the principle (of harmony) was true only to a limited degree and under especially favorable circumstances. These circumstances were not present in the context of monopoly capitalism. Various strategies have been attempted to remedy the problem, but most have ended in totalitarianism (fascist or communist). For Tillich, the imperative need of the "world situation" was to shun these false remedies without accepting the illness itself: that is, to avoid "both totalitarian absolutism and [extreme] liberal individualism." In terms of economic organization, the basic question for him was this: "Shall humankind return to the monopolistic structure from which our present economic, political and psychological disintegration has resulted?" Or else this: "Shall humankind go forward to an integrated economy which is neither totalitarian nor in the service of war?" Here the idea of religious socialism resolutely makes its comeback. "Christianity," Tillich writes, "must support plans for economic reorganization which promise to overcome the antithesis of [totalitarian] absolutism and [selfish] individualism"; it must insist "that the virtually infinite productive capacities of humankind shall be used for the advantage of everyone, instead of being restricted and wasted for the profit interests of a controlling minority." Moving beyond the domestic economic context, Tillich's text stressed the relevance of religious socialism also in the broad global arena by pointing a way beyond clashing national sovereignties. Just as a reflectively shared "way of life" was needed domestically, the cultivation of a "common spirit" also was required to sustain the world beyond exploitation and domination.[29]

Religious Socialism or Barbarism

In its appeal to humankind, Tillich's text of 1945 was stirring and fully in accord with the demands of propheticism. Here is a sentence that deserves to be lifted up—and to be repeated and reaffirmed seventy years later: "Christianity must declare that, in the next period of history, those political forms are right which are able to produce and maintain a community in which chronic fear of a miserable and meaningless life for the masses is abolished, and in which everyone participates creatively in the self-realization of the community, whether local, national, regional, or international." What needs to be added is that, already in the cited text, Tillich did not entrust the fostering of a future community solely to Christian churches; in a genuinely "ecumenical" and even cosmopolitan spirit, he was ready to enlist other world religions and indeed all ethical orientations in the common global endeavor. As the conclusion of the text stated: "The Christian church can speak authoritatively and effectively in our world today only if it is truly 'ecumenical,' that is, universal."[30] One of the prominent features of the remaining decades of Tillich's life was precisely this ecumenical or cosmopolitan outreach, manifest in his growing preoccupation with the teachings of non-Western religious and philosophical traditions. A particularly noteworthy episode—somewhat unsettling for the Christian theologian—was his sustained encounter with Zen Buddhism. But this encounter was only one illustration of his broader engagement with the prospect of a future world community.[31]

During much of the postwar period, Tillich refrained again from actively participating in public life in his new homeland.[32] In fact, he committed himself strongly, and almost exclusively, to his theological work, especially the elaboration of his *magnum opus*, *Systematic Theology* (whose first volume was published in 1951, its second in 1957, and its third and final volume in 1963). To be sure, devoting himself to theological work did not mean in Tillich's case a complete retreat from the world—something that would have gone against the very grain of his theology: his (dialectical) linkage of faith and culture. What his "systematic" work entailed was not a shunning of worldly ties but a strengthening of the prophetic dimension of genuine faith.

Thus the hope for a future world community was increasingly and emphatically couched in the language of prophetic expectation: the promise of the "Kingdom of God"—a promise that had been eloquently invoked in Tillich's essay of 1938 in these words: "The Kingdom of God is the dynamic fulfillment of the ultimate meaning of existence against the contradictions [and demonic derailments] of existence." The same promise had remained a recessed *leitmotiv* in all his later writings. It surged forth powerfully in the final part of the last volume of *Systematic Theology*, which carries the title "History and the Kingdom of God."[33]

As is clear from preceding discussions, the Kingdom of God and history in Tillich's thought are linked in a tensional relation. Simply put: the Kingdom is not simply an event in worldly history, nor is it purely otherworldly: if it were part of history, if it would lose its character as prophetic judgment; if it were otherworldly, it would lose its quality as a promise for humanity. Stressing his dialectical approach, Tillich writes: The Kingdom "has an inner-historical and a trans-historical side. As inner-historical, it participates in the dynamics of history; as trans-historical, it addresses the ambiguities of this dynamics." Differently stated: the Kingdom holds immanence and transcendence in delicate balance. The same delicate balance is also captured in the expression "history of salvation," an expression that points to "a sequence of events in which saving power breaks into historical processes—prepared for by these processes so that it can be received—changing them to enable the saving power to be effective in history." In salvation history, sacred and secular dimensions converge in the sense that history shows its "self-transcending character," its striving toward "ultimate fulfillment." As Tillich concedes, the meeting of sacred and secular elements is not always salvific but can also lead to derailments, especially the absorption of the sacred by the "world." Throughout the centuries, this has often happened in Christian churches. These churches, he states, "which represent the Kingdom of God in its fight against the forces of profanation and demonization, are themselves subject to the ambiguities of history and thus open to profanation and demonization." Here resolute liberating struggles are needed and have been fought on many occasions: "Such fights can lead to reformation movements, and it is the fact of such movements which gives the churches some right to consider themselves vehicles of the Kingdom of God, struggling in history."[34]

As should be clear, salvation history is not just the history of Christianity or Christian churches but the ultimate meaning of the history of humanity as a whole. Here Tillich returns to his deeper dialectical reflections (partly inspired by Schelling): on the distinction between essence and existence, between original "ground" and ultimate end. Seen in these terms, human history means the movement from the pure potency of "being" to steadily intensified existential actualization. This move to actuality, however, brings with it the countermove of ambiguity: the danger of "demonic" diremptions and derailments. This danger engenders the desire for a "return to origins"—but this return is blocked by the upsurge of the repressive (or "negative") side of the origin. Hence, the salvific road is one of transformation through and beyond actuality, thus moving from original potency to a higher potency, from original enabling "being" to a purified or "New Being," from "temporal" to "eternal life." Once the Kingdom of God is viewed as the "end of history," Tillich writes, one perceives that "the ever present 'end of history' elevates the positive [enabling] content of history into eternity at the same time that it excludes the negative [demonic] from participating in it. . . . Eternal life, then, includes the positive content of history, liberated from its negative distortions and fulfilled in its potentialities." History here is general or universal "*human* history," though with a prophetic proviso: "The transition from the temporal to the eternal, the 'end' of the temporal, is not a temporal event—just as creation is not a temporal event. Time is the form of the created finite, and eternity is the inner aim, the *telos* of creation, permanently elevating the finite into itself."[35]

The image of the Kingdom of God, as invoked by Tillich, is profoundly gripping and elevating. So is his portrayal of eternal or divine life—which he says is marked by "eternal blessedness," though it is achieved through "fight and victory." Before getting carried away by this portrayal, however, one should remember that Tillich was never an airy utopian neglectful of real-life calamities and experiences. The entire course of his life was overshadowed by dramatic calamities and "demonic" or near-demonic historical derailments. Thus in his work the blessed life in the Kingdom is silhouetted against the backdrop of immensely destructive, life-denying forces, especially the Apocalyptic danger of the nuclear destruction of the world. Already at the end of World War II, Tillich joined the Commission on Christian Conscience and Weapons of Mass Destruction, a group that denounced as unacceptable and "demonic" the idea of launching "preventive war" in the absence of aggression. The commission also pleaded strongly against any "first use" of nuclear weapons and any military action that, in the unfolding Cold War, would drive the superpowers into nuclear confrontation.[36] In some of his own speeches and writings during the postwar period, Tillich rejected the idea of a "just" nuclear war, arguing that starting a war with the intent of using nuclear weapons was both illegitimate and foolish (because there can be no "winnable nuclear war"). In 1954, partly on the urging of the National Committee for a Sane Nuclear Policy (SANE), he wrote a forceful indictment of the "hydrogen bomb" that included these statements: "The increasing and apparently unlimited power of the means of self-destruction in human hands puts before us the question of the ultimate meaning of this development. . . . Everyone who is aware of the possibility of humankind's self-destruction must resist this possibility to the utmost: For life and history have an eternal dimension."[37]

What emerges here, now on a global level, is the stark opposition evoked at the end of *The Socialist Decision*: the opposition between "socialism (religiously conceived) and barbarism." The most stirring condemnation of the demonic conflict unleashed in our time was written by Tillich soon after the war, when the world was still under the immediate impact of Hiroshima and Nagasaki; it is called "The Shaking of the Foundations." The text is preceded by citations from Jeremiah and Isaiah, especially this citation (Isaiah 24:18–19): "The foundations of the earth do shake. Earth breaks to pieces, is split into pieces, shakes to pieces. Earth reels like a drunken man, rocks like a hammock." As Tillich comments: the prophets described with visionary power what a great number of human beings have experienced in our time and "what, perhaps in the not too distant future, all humankind will experience abundantly." Thus the visions of the prophets have become "an actual, physical possibility," and the phrase "Earth is split into pieces" is not a poetic metaphor but "a hard reality" today: "This is the religious meaning of the age into which we have entered." To be sure, there have always been destructive forces in the world, but in the past they were constrained and more than counter-balanced by enabling potencies. Thus the "unruly power" of the world was bound up by "cohesive structures"; the "fiery chaos of the beginning" was transformed into "the fertile soil of the earth." But in modernity something happened: humankind has discovered the key to "unlock the forces of the ground," that is, incredibly destructive forces. Human beings have subjected "the basis of life and thought to *their* will"—and they "willed destruction." This is "why the founda-tions of the earth rock and shake in our time."[38]

To some extent, it was modern science that enabled humanity to unlock the "forces of the ground." But, Tillich adds, it was not science as enabling knowledge, as self-critical inquiry. Rather, it was science wedded to a "hidden idolatry," to a belief in the earth as "the place for the establishment of the Kingdom of God" and in ourselves as "the agents through whom this was to be achieved." It was this idolatrous science, preaching the bliss of humanly fabricated "prog-ress," that gave to humanity "the power to annihilate itself and the world." Unfortunately, preachers of earthly bliss usually find open or receptive ears, while prophetic voices pointing to dangers ahead tend to be shunned. Often prophetic voices are denounced as heralds of doom and sometimes even called disloyal or unpatriotic. How-ever, Tillich asks, "Is it a sign of patriotism or of confidence in one's people, its institutions and ways of life, to be silent when the foun-dations are shaking? Is the expression of optimism, whether justi-fied or not, really more valuable than the expression of truth, even if the truth is deep and dark?" At this point, Tillich addresses himself directly to his readers and hearers, issuing an urgent wake-up call: "In which of these groups do you belong—among those who respond to the prophetic spirit, or among those who close their ears and hearts to it?" His text leaves no doubt about his own position and commit-ments. "In these days," he concludes, when "the foundations of the earth *do* shake," let us "*not* turn our eyes away; let us *not* close our ears and our mouths! But may we rather see, through the crumbling of a world, the rock of eternity and the salvation which has no end."[39]

Tillich's plea, I believe, still addresses us today. The dangers or calamities of which he warned have not ceased or disappeared; on the contrary, our world today is inundated with a massive avalanche of calamities and disasters. Wherever one looks, one finds turbulence, mayhem, orgies of bloodshed, an array of wars, proxy wars, hybrid wars. In the midst of all this, there is the emergence of something like a new Cold War, pitting against each other superpowers armed to the teeth with nuclear weapons in a confrontation in which the smallest miscalculation can produce apocalypse.[40] And behind this there is the division or "splitting" of the world into hostile classes, races, tribes, and religions. Do we not already hear the rumbling of the "shaking of the foundations"? In this situation, what will be our position? Will we close or open our hearts and minds? Are we still willing to listen to Tillich's summons? As we should note, Tillich's is a prophetic but also a gentle voice; it is not a shrill voice hankering for Armageddon. As Ronald Stone says correctly: Tillich maintained trust in the Kingdom of God which comes "through acts of truth, love, and caring commitment." His hope was not for the privileged and "exceptional" few but for a "reunion with God and *all* of creation." As far as worldly life in history is concerned (Stone adds), he continued to believe in "his vision of a moderate, democratic religious socialism." It was to him the best antidote to the mounting dangers of a new barbarism and also the most promising avenue toward justice and global peace if pursued with faithful expectation.[41]

Chapter Two

Sacred Secularity

Raimon Panikkar's Holistic Faith

I am not second to anybody in the thirst for justice.
—Raimon Panikkar, *A Self-Critical Dialogue*

According to a well-known biblical passage, those with religious faith are meant to be "the salt of the earth" (Matthew 5:13). The phrase signifies that faith and worldly life (or life on "earth") are closely correlated and interdependent—though not in the mode of a seamless blend or synthesis. At the same time, being interdependent, they have a relationship that is not marked by stark antinomy or opposition. If the latter were true, religious faith would evaporate into idle fantasy or daydreaming, and worldly life would decay into rampant selfishness or moral indifference. In either sense, the "salt" mentioned in the passage would lose its "saltiness," that is, the capacity to challenge and transform existing conditions in the world. Seen from this angle, the biblical phrase suggests that faith and world are locked in an ongoing mutual challenge and contestation—such that faith stimulates the search for better or higher possibilities while itself responding to real-life exigencies. As indicated before, the theologian Paul Tillich spoke in this context of a "dialectical" relationship (using the term not in a purely logical but in an existential sense). In a similar vein, the Spanish-Indian thinker Raimon Panikkar uses the expression "sacred secularity" as a central category of his work—insisting that the phrase denotes neither a compact synthesis nor a contradiction in terms.

Given the centrality of the expression "sacred secularity," Panikkar can rightly be described as a "holistic" thinker. The propriety of the label is further underscored by another phrase that serves as a recurrent *leitmotiv* in his writings: the phrase "cosmotheandric" or "theandrocosmic" vision, which links together closely the dimensions of the divine, the human, and the natural/material (or the categories of God, humanity, and nature). However, care must be taken not to misconstrue Panikkar's "holism" in the sense of an empirical, objectifiable framework or totality. This misconstrual is obviated or radically blocked by his recurrent emphasis on the role of "difference," more specifically of "symbolic difference" (a notion loosely patterned on Martin Heidegger's "ontic-ontological" difference). This means that Panikkar's holism should never be seen as a finished system or life at rest but rather as a dynamic (temporal and transtemporal) movement—or what he elsewhere has called the "rhythm of Being."[1] In the following I want to explore this tensional holistic perspective in several contexts. First I turn to an issue that has preoccupied Panikkar from his earliest writings: the relation between religious faith or worship and the modern "secular" age. Next I move on to a theme with which Panikkar is closely (sometimes almost exclusively) identified: the theme of interreligious and cross-cultural pluralism and its *telos*. Finally I reflect on the tension prevailing in his (and any) dynamic holism: the tension between affirmation and critique or between "world confidence" and propheticism.

Worship and the Secular World

It is in the juxtaposition of religious faith and modern secularism that Panikkar's holistic or "relational" perspective surges most clearly and most immediately into view. In opposition to a widespread assumption of radical antimony, his perspective stresses the mutual embroilment of the respective terms; viewed from this angle, modern secularism or secularization appears not so much as the denial of faith as rather a new window for glimpsing the divine "through a glass darkly." This outlook was clearly spelled out in one of his early texts titled *Worship and Secular Man* (1973). At the beginning of this text, he briskly stated his approach: "To put forward my thesis straight away, only worship can prevent secularization from becoming inhuman, and only secularization can save worship from being meaningless." With this statement Panikkar aligns himself with one of the crucial philosophical and theological developments of the twentieth century: the removal of the sacred from a purely transtemporal or extraworldly sphere and the recognition of mundane temporal experience as a possible site of worship (a recognition evident, for example, in Tillich's linkage of faith and "culture"). To be sure, the encounter of faith and the secular world is not easily managed. In fact, as Panikkar notes, a mutual "total risk" emerges: namely, faith may wish to "eliminate or anathematize secularization as the main evil confronting humanity," while secularism may try to "get rid of worship as being a remnant of an age dead and gone." This risk has played itself out on many levels in modern (Western) culture and its "culture wars." What is needed to overcome existing dichotomies is nothing less than a paradigm shift or a move to a new axial or "kairological" awareness (to use Tillich's term).[2]

To make headway in this direction, Panikkar first of all elucidates and reformulates some of the key terms employed. On the one hand, he states, "worship" in this context means (or should mean) a "human action symbolizing a belief" or, more precisely, "a symbolic act arising from a particular belief" (where "symbolic" carries a quasi-transcendental or ontological significance). On the other hand, "secularism" can be traced to the Latin *saeculum*, denoting a particular world age (in the sense of *aion* or *kairos*). To this extent, the term "secular" designates the "temporal world" or the "temporal aspect of reality," whose status varies with the assessment of temporality. Once these formulations are accepted, distinct consequences follow. If time and temporality are viewed negatively (as in much of traditional philosophy), *saeculum* means the "merely" mundane and transient world as distinct from the sacred and eternal world; by contrast, if temporality is positively valued, *saeculum* will stand as a symbol for the effort of regaining or reasserting the integrity of the mundane world—an integrity previously monopolized by the "sacred" or religious realm. It is here that the need for a paradigm shift comes into play. As Panikkar writes, with characteristic verve: "Now, what is emerging in our days, and what may be a 'hapax phenomenon,' a unique occurrence in the history of humankind, is—paradoxically—not secularism, but the sacred quality of secularism." Differently phrased: "What seems to be unique in the human constellation of the present *kairos* is the disruption of the equation sacred = nontemporal with the positive value so far attached to it. The temporal is seen today as positive and, in a way, as sacred."[3]

The revaluation of temporality or the temporal world, in Panikkar's account, is linked with an important reinterpretation of human existence: a shift from the traditional conception of "animal with reason" (*animal rationale*) to that of a symbolic or symbolizing being (*homo symbolicus*), denoting a distinctive mode of existence open to, or standing out into the meaning of, reality (or Being). In a phrase deliberately patterned on Heideggerian teachings, Panikkar speaks of "symbolic difference," indicating a differential entwinement of symbol and reality—an entwinement that allows him to say that "reality discloses itself only as a symbol," with the result that "what reality *is*, is its symbol." With regard to human experience, symbolic difference means that secular "being-in-the-world" is genuine only in an "ekstatic" mode that reaches out to "the other pole, the other shore." This aspect inevitably puts pressure on secularization, revealing it as a "constitutively ambivalent" process: on the one hand, it can erode or destroy traditional forms of worship; on the other, it can transform, purify, and renew them. Against this background, the basic aim of his book—Panikkar observes—is to affirm "the liturgical nature" of human existence, thus treating worship as an essential feature of human life while at the same time recognizing secularity as an integral character of the present and the impending future. Today, he adds, "anyone who is not exposed to secularization cannot hope to realize his/her humanity to the full. . . . On the other hand, human life without worship cannot even [ontologically] subsist."[4]

In addition to stressing the symbolic quality of experience, *Worship and Secular Man* offers broader reflections on secularization silhouetted against the history of Western metaphysics. According to Panikkar, this history can be conveniently grouped and expounded under three "kairological moments": heteronomy, autonomy, and ontonomy (which can be seen as variations on Tillich's categories of heteronomy, autonomy, and theonomy). In Panikkar's usage, "heteronomy" designates a worldview that relies on a hierarchical structure of reality regulating all things from above, while "autonomy" insists on radical human self-reliance, individual inquiry, and self-determination; "ontonomy" finally refers to a perspective shunning both external and internal constitution and accentuating instead a holistic web of (ontological) relationships. Ontonomy, Panikkar states, means "the realization of the *nomos* of being" at the profound level "where unity does not impinge on diversity"; it rests on the *specular* character of reality, "where each part mirrors the whole" in a refracted way. Sharply deviating from celebrations of hierarchy (on the part of religious or political reactionaries), Panikkar charges heteronomy with denuding or desacralizing the world in favor of official authority or authoritarianism (sometimes culminating in theocracy or caesaropapism). In Western history, the Renaissance and the Reformation ushered in the age of "profane autonomy," which privileged the state over the church, science over philosophy, and the "profane" over the "sacred." As the text astutely notes, autonomy in the last analysis is always "a reaction against heteronomy," that is, a rebellion "against the abuses of the heteronomic structure." In the Enlightenment and its aftermath, there was still a limited place for God, but "for a God who respects the rules of the game, a God (as it were) whose nature and attributes I discover and in a sense postulate." Above all, the divine here was radically privatized and reduced to a target of subjective choice or preference.[5]

In Panikkar's account, what is coming into view in our late-modern age—partly as a result of secularization—is the perspective of a "theandric" or "cosmotheandric" ontonomy that stresses the integral though differentiated connection among the divine, the human, and nature (or the cosmos). What this outlook opposes, above all, are traditional metaphysical dualisms or dichotomies: "The field of the sacred is no longer defined in opposition to that of the secular, nor is a development of worship made at the cost of work, politics or any other human activity." Human beings in this view are considered neither as sovereign agents nor as passive victims of authority but rather as participants in the ongoing disclosure or epiphany of "being," in the effort of a *consecratio mundi* pervading the deepest strands of reality. Whereas heteronomy typically views secularization as a "blasphemous" enterprise soiling the garment of hierarchical authority and whereas autonomy greets secularization as the "grand achievement" of modernity and the "greatest victory for the liberation of man," ontonomy construes the same process in a different light: namely, as the tapping of the hidden potential or promise of the world. In doing so, Panikkar comments, ontonomy seeks to "enlighten our vision," to make us realize "that the worship that matters is the worship *of* the secular world"—where the latter phrase means "worship *of* (possessed by, coming from, corresponding and fitting to) this secular world."[6]

About a decade after writing *Worship and Secular Man*, Panikkar returned to the topic of secularization and the meaning of secularity, focusing more specifically on the relation between faith and political life. In the new text, titled "Religion or Politics: The Western Dilemma," the earlier notion of "symbolic difference" was modified or amplified by a further differential entwinement. According to Panikkar, the history of Western civilization has been dominated by two contrasting models: either religion and politics have been fused, leading to forms of theocracy or caesaropapism, or they have been separated and pitted against each other "as if religion and politics were mutually incompatible and antagonistic forces." The first model gives rise to such dangers as religious opportunism, fundamentalism, and even variants of totalitarianism; in the second model, favored by agnostics and "all types of liberalisms," separation readily leads to degeneracy in politics by reducing it to a "mere application of techniques." Invoking again the perspective of ontonomy, Panikkar sees our age (or *saeculum*) as capable of moving beyond the "Western dilemma" of monism/dualism or immanence/transcendence. As he notes, various developments in our time warrant the conclusion that "we are approaching the close of the modern Western dichotomy between religion and politics, and we are coming nearer to a 'non-dualistic' relation between the two"—where nondualism is a translation of the Indian notion of *Advaita*. Elaborating further on this point, he states: "The relationship can also be *ontonomous*, that is to say, it can be one of constitutive interdependence regulated by the very nature of both religion and politics as being two elements of the same [*advaitic*] human reality." This outlook rescues both terms from mutual negation and isolation—an isolation predicated on the assumption that religion is "only concerned with the divine, the supernatural, the eternal, the sacred," while politics is confined to "the earthly, the natural, the profane." Moving beyond both segregation and fusion, *advaitic* ontonomy teaches: "God and the world are not two realities, nor are they one and the same. . . . There is no politics separate from religion; there is no religious factor that is not at the same time a political factor. . . . The divine tabernacle is to be found among men; the earthly city is a divine happening."[7]

Cultural Pluralism and Disarmament

Panikkar's holistic outlook is not limited to the metaphysical or the ontological domain of "cosmotheandrism." Partly under the impact of globalization and its offshoots, Panikkar extended this perspective also to the lateral relations between different cultures and religions. A major stepping stone in this direction was his study *The Intra-Religious Dialogue* (1978), which could also have been called *The Inter-Religious* (and even *The Cross-Cultural*) *Dialogue*, since the focus was not placed on discussions inside a particular religion or culture. As in the case of cosmotheandrism, the basic issue for Panikkar was how to avoid both the rigid separation or divorce and the seamless blending or amalgamation of life forms (that is, how to steer beyond both monism and dualism). With regard to interreligious encounters, the study distinguishes the alternatives of "exclusivism" and "inclusivism," adding as a third (equally flawed) option the scheme of "parallelism." The first type of exclusivism is based on the absolute truth claim of a given religion, for "if a certain tradition claims to offer a universal context of truth, anything contrary to that 'universal truth' will have to be declared false." As an alternative to exclusion, the absolute truth of one's faith can be safeguarded through inclusivism; as Panikkar writes: "The most plausible condition for the claim to truth of one's own tradition is to affirm at the same time that it includes at different levels all that there is of truth wherever it exists." Accordingly, this attitude will reinterpret things in such a way as to make them "not only palatable but also assimilable" (that is, reducible to oneness). The third option of parallelism assumes that religious creeds, although different, "actually run parallel to meet only in the ultimate"; while stressing the "self-sufficiency of every tradition," it denies "the need or (in)convenience of mutual learning."[8]

For Panikkar, none of these options is appealing because they all undercut a genuine (though differential) relationship; the dangers of rejection, co-optation, and indifference are too great. Hence, a new way has to be found. In his words: "The aim of intrareligious encounter is understanding; it is *not* to win over the other or to come to a total agreement." Understanding presupposes communication, and the latter requires acceptance of a diversity of languages and traditions. Crisply put: "Pluralism stands between unrelated plurality and a monolithic unity." As one should note here, genuine pluralism for Panikkar is sharply distinguished from "plurality," denoting the mere juxtaposition of beliefs. The distinction is captured by the notion of "dialogue" seen as the lifeblood connecting different religious (and cultural) contexts. His study is eloquent in capturing the virtues of dialogue. A crucial requisite is a radical openness to the "other," a willingness to undergo a basic learning experience. As he writes, a dialogue (especially a religious dialogue) "must first of all be an *authentic* dialogue, without superiority, preconceptions, hidden motives or convictions on either side. . . . It must preclude preconceiving its aims and results." Encountering others in this dialogical sense can be traumatic and upsetting: "It runs the risk of modifying my ideas, my most personal horizons, the very framework of my life." At another point, in order to contrast dialogue with both empty chitchat and purely logical arguments, Panikkar uses the notion of a "dialogical dialogue," stating: "This dialogical dialogue, which differs from a dialectical one, stands on the assumption that nobody has access to the universal horizon of human experience, and that only by *not* postulating the rules of the encounter from a single side can human existence proceed toward a deeper and more universal understanding of itself and come closer to self-realization."[9]

As can readily be seen, dialogical pluralism is exposed to a number of pitfalls or derailments threatening its holistic quality, especially the pitfalls of relativism (devoid of truth) and absolutism (imposing a unitary truth). In Panikkar's presentation, the difference between plurality and pluralism corresponds to that between relativism and genuine relationism or "relativity." As he writes, dialogue "overcomes the temptation of *relativism* by acknowledging *relativity*. Instead of everything falling into an agnostic or indifferent relativism, everything is wrapped in a relativity of radical interdependence because every being is a function in the order of beings and has its own place in the dynamism of history." The other derailment (perhaps even more prominent in our time) is that of universal co-optation or inclusion. This danger is evident in contemporary interreligious or interfaith encounters and even in the global movement of "ecumenism." Panikkar writes: "The great temptation for ecumenism is to extrapolate, that is, to use a native growth [or tradition] beyond the bounds of its native soil. We all have seen what comes of exporting European and American democracy" or ideological belief systems. Becoming more concrete or explicit, the text speaks of the danger of ideological colonialism or imperialism. "The encounter of religions today," we read, "is vital for the religious life of contemporary humanity." However, in the meeting of cultures and religions, the "time for one-way traffic" is today passé, despite "powerful vestiges of a past colonialist attitude." Crisply stated: "Neither monologue nor conquest is tenable. The *spolia aegyptorum* mentality is no longer possible nor in any way justifiable. To think that one people, one culture, one religion has the right—or the duty for that matter—to dominate all the rest belongs to a past period in world history."[10]

Unhappily, the preceding statement was too optimistic or irenic—as Panikkar soon discovered. Increasingly he came to realize the persisting danger of cultural monologue, of the *spolia aegyptorum* mentality cultivated on behalf or for the benefit of a dominant or hegemonic worldview. This realization or apprehension surfaced eloquently in some essays he published less than a decade after *The Intra-Religion Dialogue*, especially in his paper "The Invisible

Harmony: A Universal Theory of Religion or a Cosmic Confidence in Reality?" (1987). By that time, the weakening and progressive dismantling of the Soviet Union had spawned in many quarters the vision of an "end of history," of the culmination of historical developments in a final synthesis represented by a universal system or world state. Intellectually, the time gave rise to the formulation of global or universal "theories" of everything and the establishment of centers of "global" or world affairs (all wedded to monologue). Panikkar's essay resolutely challenged these initiatives, perceiving them (correctly) as modes of hegemonic "globalization from above." He wrote, "Under the notion of 'universal theory,' I encompass all those efforts at reaching a 'global' intellectual understanding, be it called 'ecumenical Esperanto,' 'world theology,' 'world philosophy,' 'unified field theory', or even a certain [monological] type of 'comparative religion' and 'ecumenism.'" The common trait of all these conceptions, he added, is "the noble effort of reducing the immense variety of human experience to one single and common language" by subsuming them all under a uniform structure of rationality. For Panikkar, the thrust toward universality had been "a feature of Western civilization since the Greeks." Universal rule was the motto of the Spaniards' conquest, and following it the Spaniards reached America eventually giving rise to a plethora of formulas: "World government, planetary culture, universal net of information, world market, the universal value of technology, nation states, human rights and so on—all pointing to the same global principle."[11]

For Panikkar, the striving for universality is not entirely illegitimate because it promises a certain orderliness and hence intelligibility of phenomena. The latter desire is particularly prominent in our time given the present information overload. Never before in human history, he writes, "have we had so much information available regarding the ways in which our fellow human beings live and have lived." As a result, we are now "submerged in an avalanche of data," and the need for intelligibility becomes powerful. In the face of this avalanche, there is no longer a possibility of retreating into local parochialism and regaining the simplicity of the past, such as "the innocence of the Amerindian tribes who assumed that others worship more or less the same Great Spirit." Although conceding this point, Panikkar perceives grave danger in the thrust toward universality, pretty much along Nietzschean lines. "The very trend of looking for 'universal theory,' even if expressed with all the respect and openness possible," he writes, "betrays the same *forma mentis*, the continuation of the same thrust—the will to understand which is also a form of the will to power, and thus of the felt need to have everything under control." Quite apart from and in addition to this Nietzschean reservation, the drive toward universalism is intrinsically flawed or misleading, first because it cannot deliver a coherently universal "*theory*" (rationality being of many different kinds) and, second, because no theory can be exhaustive or fully encompassing (due to the lack of a total overview or an absolute Archimedean point).[12]

What mainly concerns Panikkar is the underside of globalism or universalism. Although perhaps expressing "the genius of the West," he states, "we do not any longer want intellectual colonialism." In order to make its claim, universalism has to employ a "*lingua universalis*" that does not exist or at least amounts to a radical reductionism. At this point, Panikkar turns again to the centrality of pluralism, properly conceived. "Pluralism in its ultimate sense," he writes, "is not the tolerance of a diversity of systems under a larger umbrella; it does not allow for any superstructure. It is not a supersystem." Adopting an outlook akin to that of Adorno's "negative dialectics," the text here articulates a dialectical correlation devoid of final synthesis or fusion: "Pluralism has to do with final unbridgeable human attitudes. If two views allow for a synthesis, we cannot speak of pluralism. . . . We do not take seriously the claim of the ultimacy of religions, philosophies, theologies, and human attitudes if we seem to allow for a 'pluralistic' supersystem." In an effort to avoid the abyss of nihilism and complete unintelligibility, Panikkar (as on earlier occasions) resorts to the distinction between "relativism" and "relationality" and finally to the bridge-building function of dialogue radically construed. "Relativism," he observes, "destroys itself when affirming that all is relative and thus also the very affirmation of relativism. Relativity, on the other hand, asserts that any human affirmation, and thus any truth, is relative to its very own parameters and that there can be no ab-solute truth, for truth is relational" (that is, related to the human condition). In the move from relativism to relativity, what is required is a radical "openness" of the participants, that is, a willingness to abandon familiar parochialisms while venturing through dialogue into the unfamiliar terrain of new learning experiences. As previously indicated, dialogue—in the sense of "dialogical dialogue"—involves not merely logical argumentation but also an existential transformation.[13]

As can be seen, Panikkar's thought does not entirely reject a global perspective but insists on proceeding laterally or from the ground up. This emphasis on lateral learning is also the trademark of his conception of "comparative" philosophy and theology—where he replaces the Latin "*comparare*" with the term "*imparare*," meaning learning or acquiring new insights. As Panikkar writes in the discussed text: "Strictly speaking, comparative religion is not possible, because we do not have any neutral platform outside every tradition whence comparison may be drawn.... We cannot compare (*comparare*), for there is no fulcrum outside. We can only *imparare*, that is, learn from the other, opening ourselves from our standpoint to a dialogical dialogue that does not seek to win or to convince, but to search together from our different vantage points." Unfortunately, he adds, there is today still a powerful hankering for a global fulcrum, backed up by hegemonic "military-industrial" agendas. "The political and economic situation of the world today," he states bluntly, "compels us to radical changes in our conception of humanity and the place of humanity in the cosmos. The present system seems to be running toward major catastrophes of all kinds." To be sure, the changes endorsed by Panikkar cannot take the form of unilateral machinations or "revolutions" (especially violent revolutions)—given the propensity of unilateralism to succumb to the Nietzschean "will to power" or the will to dominate. What is required is something entirely different—what Panikkar calls a "cosmic trust" guided by a "new innocence." He writes, "What is needed is trust, a certain trust that sustains a common struggle for an ever better shaping of reality." As the very word (especially the Latin *fiducia*) suggests, "this trust entails a certain 'fidelity' to oneself, 'con-fidence' in the world as cosmos, 'loyalty' in the struggle itself, a basic 'belief' in the human endeavor, or rather in the sort of worthwhile collaboration of humans in the overall adventure of being."[14]

Invoking this notion of trust did not entirely silence Panikkar's apprehension about hegemonic globalism. In fact, that apprehension resurfaced powerfully barely a decade later in a text titled *Cultural Disarmament: The Way to Peace* (1995). As one can surmise, the book was at least in part triggered by the aftermath of the collapse of the Soviet Union, a period that gave rise in some quarters to a virulent triumphalism wedded to a monological, Western-centric "world order." Above anything else, the book was a fervent defense of peace equaling in stature and philosophical depth older classical texts (like those of Cusanus and Erasmus). For Panikkar, peace is not simply a political arrangement, the termination of warfare through "conflict resolution" or peace treaties; rather, like warfare or bloodshed, it reaches into religious or spiritual depths. More simply put, peace overarches the difference between mundane-political and religious-spiritual dimensions. Taking some cues from his notion of "sacred secularity," Panikkar writes that secularity (in his sense) "enables us to discover the religious dimension of political peace, without falling victim to theocracy. The *pax civilis* is the indispensable constituent of the *pax religiosa*, and vice versa"—which is a "nondualistic [*advaitic*] thesis." Digging still more deeply into spiritual roots, Panikkar emphasizes that genuine peace cannot be humanly manufactured, nor can it be imposed from outside or above; it is a "gift" that must be properly received and cultivated. In his words: "Peace puts us on notice: the will in this area is not sovereign [or autonomous]. I cannot give myself peace." Thus peace does not come from ourselves, as the outcome of our will; but neither does it come from others: "It does not flourish in the kingdom of heteronomy." In the Christian tradition, peace is a fruit of the "Spirit."[15]

As indicated before, *Cultural Disarmament* is a treatise on peace of a nearly classical stature. An opening chapter charts a pathway toward a "philosophy of peace" (*philosophia pacis*) seen as a corrective to a purely "analytical" approach treating peace as a quasi-empirical object. That chapter presents a series of "*sutras*" (observations) that in their interrelation provide insight into "the precious thing we call peace." The first *sutra* states that peace is "participation in the harmony of the rhythm of being," where "harmony" does not mean absence of differences and even polarities but rather their nonviolent relationship. As Panikkar writes (in a Gandhian spirit), nonviolence does not signify mere aloofness or passivity but "the non-violation of personhood, the engaged celebration of the profound dignity of every being." Another *sutra* insists on the interconnection of "outer" and "inner" realms: "The absence of *inner* peace foments cold wars and opens the way for conflicts unleashing all manners of revenge. . . . Yet without *outer* peace, inner peace is but a chimera, an exclusively psychological state of isolation from the rest of reality." Recalling that peace cannot be fabricated or manufactured or imposed on or by others, a further *sutra* comments: "We discover peace, we unveil it; it is a discovery, not a conquest, the fruit of a re-velation." Finally there is the realization that "victory never leads to peace": "In the words of Simone Weil, peace is a fugitive that has escaped the victor's camp." A later chapter develops a complex trilogy (or trinity) in which peace involves a synergy of freedom, justice, and harmony. "Freedom" here means not just *liberum arbitrium* or "freedom of choice" but rather an existential condition making room for "doing, thinking, acting, in conformity with what or who one is." "Justice," in turn, does not coincide with legal order but reflects an ontological "fitting-ness" (captured by the Indian notion of *dharma*). "Harmony" finally denotes a holistic concord "among all sectors of reality."[16]

Given the elevated status of Panikkar's conception, the reader cannot fail to notice the enormous distance separating it from our present world (often termed the "nuclear age"). Panikkar is quite aware of this distance. As he notes, "The idea of peace, too, can degenerate." He cites two prominent historical examples: the *pax Romana* and *pax Americana*: "The former was based on belief in the protection of the 'civilized world' from the barbarians. The lat-ter attempts to justify itself with similar arguments, appealing to the defense of democracy and 'free trade.'" The root cause of strife is always a warlike disposition fostered by culture—including Western culture(s). "Our cultures," Panikkar states, in a sharply critical spirit, "are customarily belligerent and treat others as enemies, barbarians, *goi*, *mleccha*, *khafir*, pagans, infidels, and the like." Enhancing the strain of cultural dissidence, he adds: "It is not by pure chance that Western civilization has developed such an arsenal of weapons, in quality as well as quantity. There is something inherent in this culture that has brought us to this pass: our competitiveness, our tendency to keep thinking up 'better solutions,' . . . our superiority complex, sense of universality, and so forth." Given these dispositions, the outcome is not surprising. Panikkar at this point offers a brief synopsis focusing just on recent times: "More than 1,200 victims of war have fallen daily since World War II, 2,000 a day in 1991. There are at present, and there have been for many years, more than twenty major armed conflicts in the world. The refugees in the world number in the millions, just as do orphaned, starving, and street children." What makes things still worse is that most wars wear and have worn "a religious face" or claim "religious justification."[17]

This litany of disasters, calamities, and degradations underscores the urgency of the task announced in the book's title: "cultural disarmament." The phrase clearly is meant provocatively. In Panikkar's words: "By this somewhat mordant expression, we wish to refer to the necessary interculturality of a serious effort for peace." More specifically, the expression challenges cultural hegemony ("globalism from above"); it "refers in a special way to the predominant culture which has scientific and technological character and is of European origin." Still more "mordantly," the phrase means "the abandonment of the trenches in which 'modern' culture, of Western origin, has dug in, regarding its values as vested and nonnegotiable, such as progress, technology, science, democracy, the world economic market, not to mention governmental organizations." Panikkar does not hesitate to insist on this point: "By 'cultural disarmament' or the 'disarmament of modern culture,' I mean to allude to a radical change in the predominant 'myth' of contemporary humanity—of that part of humanity that is most vociferous, influential and wealthy, and is in control of the destinies of global politics." At a later point, the study engages in the "deconstruction" of the "myth" or paradigmatic structure of modern Western culture, focusing on three main elements (seen as key "obstacles to peace"): militarism, technocracy (or technoscience), and linear developmentalism. As Panikkar recognizes, changing these structural features is enormously difficult, requiring a basic *metanoia*; but he considers the latter necessary for genuine interculturality, for the "establishment of dialogue on an equal footing with the other cultures of the earth." He also realizes that his proposal may be termed utopian. "This may be," he responds. "But aside from its value as a utopia, in this case one must reflect that the alternative is human, planetary catastrophe."[18]

Cosmic Trust and Prophetism

Panikkar's assessment of modern secular culture is grim and uncompromising. Combined, its constitutive features render that culture "unsustainable," a prime example of Nietzsche's "growing desert." Its intrinsic militarism has produced a "civilization of armed reason" whose reason is employed to create more and more deadly weapons. Thus long-distance weapons are invented whose lethal effects are divorced from human reach or sensibility; Hiroshimas are unleashed with the mere push of buttons. Technocracy more generally destroys the "human scale," leading to the replacement of the "human measure" by "the measure proper to machines." As a result, the human being is transformed from *homo loquens* into "technocratic man" and even into *homo telematicus* (remote-controlling man). Linear developmentalism, finally, predicts the extension of the modern malaise to the world at large, bringing into view the prospect of global ecological disasters and "planetary catastrophes." Small wonder that, for Panikkar, this battery of calamities calls for radical remedies, for a resolute turning-about. As he writes, these remedies cannot be found in such fictive panaceas as "atomic deterrents," "Star Wars," or a "new world order"—all based on hegemonic ideologies. Rather, the path to recovery presents a steep human challenge. "It is a revolutionary, disconcerting path, a path requiring the suppression of injustice, selfishness, greed." The difficulty is "immense."[19]

Although persuasive in its sheer urgency, Panikkar's presentation here raises important philosophical and theological issues. For, one may ask, is there any evidence of a human capacity or willingness for radical change? More important, the grim character of modern culture puts pressure on Panikkar's key notion of "sacred secularity." For what—one can query—is at all "sacred" about this secular culture? Are we not really facing here an oxymoron? At some points, Panikkar is willing to speak of "profane" secularity; but given its destructiveness, its propensity to catastrophe, is this term sufficient? Maybe one should invoke here Tillich's stronger term "demonic" and acknowledge that, in some respects, modern worldliness is abysmally countersacred. What opens up at this point is a gulf inside "sacred secularity" that it seems hard to bridge. Or can one still say that, despite demonic derailments and injustices, the world (the secular world) is still somehow hale or in God's hands? One is reminded here of a phrase of the poet Hölderlin (repeatedly invoked by Heidegger): "But where there is danger, there the saving grace (*das Rettende*) grows." Does this mean that, in the midst of Nietzsche's "growing desert" (or perhaps as its consequence), an entirely different growth takes place? Panikkar at one point invokes the puzzling stanza placed by Dante over the gates of hell: "Divine majesty, highest wisdom, basic love."[20]

In addition to raising questions of theodicy, Panikkar's portrayal of modernity—as a looming catastrophe—also puts pressure on his "holism," the irenic outlook pervading his work. Many of his comments clearly convey a sense of intense drama or tragic tension not usually associated with the notion of harmony. Hence, holism here needs to be carefully assessed. As used by Panikkar, "holism" evidently is not something that can be conceptually grasped or encompassed. This means that holism is always "ekstatic," pointing beyond itself; maybe it can be called "apophatic." At another point, Panikkar enlists for his purposes Heraclitus's statement: "Invisible harmony is stronger than the visible" (*Fragments* 54). What this phrase suggests is that harmony/holism is always dynamic, self-transgressing or on the move—a point resonating with Heidegger's teaching that "potentiality" is greater than "actuality." In a different register, the point also resonates with Tillich's emphasis on the necessarily "prophetic" quality of religious faith. One of the crucial bedrocks of Panikkar's holism is (what he calls) "cosmic trust" or "confidence," that is, trust in the ultimate wholeness or fullness (*pleroma*) of life. As he writes, this concept of plenitude is "in complete harmony with the central Christian doctrine of the *incarnation*," which expresses the *telos* of humanity and of all creation. But it now seems that this fullness also includes an absence: the cross and the experience of the "desert"—including the desert of late modernity. Thus cosmic trust cannot be trust in a finished "cosmos" but is pervaded all along by a prophetic promise or longing—which, to be sure, is not an empty daydream but is anchored (apophatically) in the foundations of the world or reality.[21]

What all of Panikkar's writings convey is that neither trust nor holism can be humanly engineered or produced. Although both involve human action or practice, the latter has to be "ontonomous" in character, that is, nurtured and sustained by spiritual engagement. An instructive example of this point is the "preferential option for the poor" favored by liberation theologians. Panikkar fully endorses this motto but gives it a special quasi-prophetic twist. As he writes, the option for the poor, for the "suffering portion of humanity," implies a challenge to the "evolutionary cosmology" underlying developmentalism (perhaps even cosmic trust). In a friendly-critical exchange, theologian Paul Knitter at one point criticized Panikkar's holistic pluralism as being perhaps too gentle and irenic, thus courting the danger of ideological obfuscation. What Knitter thought needed to be acknowledged more fully is the reigning wasteland of our age: on the social level, "the specter of poverty, starvation, malnutrition caused not by 'natural forces' but by human choices ensconced in political-economic systems"; on the global level, "the horror of wars that can devastate and have devastated vast portions of civilian populations and that, if launched with the ever-expanding nuclear arsenal, can destroy the world as we know it"; on the ecological level, "a world *already* destroyed and sacrificed on the altar of commerce and consumerism." To face up to these dismal realities, more is needed than holistic rhetoric: namely, "liberative praxis," a practical engagement for the suffering—and the "preferential option" as an exemplary mode of such praxis. Religious people involved in such praxis, Knitter adds, would form not only "base Christian communities" but "base *human* communities"—constituted by "co-pilgrims" from different backgrounds committed to the task of "*soteria*": the "struggle for justice and life."[22]

In his response, Panikkar is ready to basically second Knitter's *pathos* or ethical commitment. As he writes: "I fully share his concern. How could I not? . . . I find the justification of my life in my total dedication to justice." The only thing that troubles him is the notion of "option," which suggests a voluntary decision or autonomy;

for "any option reposes in the will, a will supposed to be free—even rational." But a life devoted to justice, service, or love relies on something stronger than options or decisions; it is a matter of "being," not choosing. In his words: "I feel I have no option but to strive for justice . . . no option but to stand at the side of the oppressed . . . no option but to speak of the truth." Traditional religious language here speaks of a vocation, of God calling, humans listening (*Shemah*). The call may come from God, but it resonates through the heart, the "innermost core of our being." These comments clearly have relevance for the notion of "cosmic trust" or "confidence." As Panikkar states (with definite prophetic and apophatic overtones): "Cosmic confidence is not trust *in* the world, confidence *in* the cosmos. [Rather,] it is the confidence *of* the cosmos itself, of which we form a part inasmuch as we simply *are*." Grammatically this is called a "subjective genitive," meaning that "the confidence itself is a cosmic fact of which we are more or less aware, and which we presuppose all the time." Ultimately, we have to trust what we experience and what we call "reality." Hence, cosmic confidence is not just "our interpretation" of the world: it is "that awareness which makes any interpretation possible in the first place." Differently put: "We cannot disclaim a cosmic order without assuming it already."[23]

As one can see, confidence for Panikkar is a "fact," but it is also a response to a calling that resonates in human life—in a heart purified to perceive the calling. Thus, to return to an earlier point: secularity may be "sacred" all along, but it discloses itself as such only to a heart that is seasoned, having traveled through the desert of our secular world and been liberated from its compulsive dross. In traditional language, purification of this kind means *metanoia*, a turning-about or cleansing that, at least tendentially, is akin to monastic conduct. Somewhere in the middle of his life, Panikkar wrote a book reflecting on that issue titled *Blessed Simplicity: The Monk as Universal Archetype*. In his presentation, "monkhood" is not a special occupation or profession reserved for particularly reclusive types; rather, it denotes a disposition that is *constitutive* of humanity as such: the disposition to care about existence and the meaning of being as such. As he writes: "By monk, I understand that person who aspires to reach the ultimate goal of life with all his being by renouncing all that is not necessary to it." In a sense, everybody is meant to strive for this ultimate meaning so that this quest is a universal human potential; the "monk" (so called) is distinguished only by the radicality of his quest. As Panikkar added: "One does not become a monk in order to do something particular or to acquire anything, but in order to *be*." The basic hypothesis articulated in the text is that "monkhood, that is, the archetype of which 'the monk' is an expression, corresponds to a dimension of the *humanum*, so that every human being has the potentiality or possibility of realizing this dimension. . . . Not everybody can or should enter a monastery, but everybody has a monastic dimension that ought to be cultivated."[24]

Given the basic character of the quest for meaning, honoring the "monastic dimension" clearly means also cultivating contemplation, mindfulness, and reflection. It means coming to one's senses to overcome the "oblivion of being" and thereby also the "abandonment of and by being" (as Heidegger called it). But contemplation, for Panikkar, is by no means a mode of solipsism, a retreat into privacy from the world as such; rather, it means a holistic recovery as a prelude to prayerful or "ontonomic" practice. As he states: Properly pursued, contemplation "leads to action." Reflection makes us aware of the suffering going on around us in the world, of people dying of hunger, being oppressed and exploited in many ways. Observing this state of affairs, Panikkar says, "I cannot leave it at that; I will have to do something. . . . The real criterion of true contemplation is that it leads to praxis, even if that praxis consists only in transforming one's own life and immediate environment." In this respect, the "monk" or the person cultivating his or her monastic capability has "the strongest moral obligation—to denounce, to cry out, to speak and to act." "Contemplation" here means consciousness-raising and civic enlightenment—which is "a dangerous activity" (as the examples of Socrates, Martin Luther King Jr., and many others demonstrate). Today, Panikkar adds, the "monk" is plunged into the cauldron of the wilderness of the world—with all the dangers this implies. If we do nothing, we become accomplices in all the miseries and injustices of the world; as accomplices "we bless and condone the status quo—which is already a political decision," as well as an abdication of our responsibility and our human calling.[25]

Cultivating our monastic vocation, in Panikkar's presentation, is not like nurturing a fixed human capacity (like universal reason). Rather, as a reflection of the ultimate meaning of life, monkhood is also responsive to the cultural and linguistic contexts of the quest. Given the embeddedness of any genuine search in language (as an attribute of *homo loquens*, not *homo telematicus*), the monastic disposition necessarily also reflects the difference of cultural and religious traditions—without making the latter a prison or fetish. In Panikkar's words: "Monasticism is not specifically a Christian, Jaina, Buddhist, or other sectarian phenomenon; it is basically a human and primordially a religious one." Nevertheless, one can practice the vocation in a Christian, Hindu, Buddhist, and even secular and atheist mode. A main reason is that "we do not speak 'language'"; rather, "when we speak, we use only one language." If this is so, Panikkar adds, "monkhood is not the monopoly of a few [monastic orders] but rather a human wellspring that may be channeled in different degrees of purity and awareness by different people in many parts of the world." As a summons to holistic awareness, responsibility, and maturity, the monastic vocation calls on all people everywhere to develop seriously—in exemplary fashion and according to their cultural contexts—the "deepest core of our humanness." When they do this, people everywhere emerge as "co-pilgrims" on the path toward a sacred secularity and *soteria*—thereby safeguarding both the natural ecological habitat and the primordial ethical-religious fiber of humanity.[26]

Chapter Three

From Desert to Bloom

Thomas Merton's Contemplative Praxis

It is my intention to make my entire life a protest against the crimes and injustices of war and political tyranny.
—Thomas Merton, *The Seven Storey Mountain*

In his *Blessed Simplicity*, Raimon Panikkar defined "monkhood" as the gravitational center of human being, as a dimension not marginal or accidental but "constitutive" of our humanity itself. As he wrote, this dimension can be channeled or developed "in different degrees of purity and awareness"; moreover, it gravitates not toward an outside or beyond but toward an inner depth where the drama of life unfolds. Viewed in this light, Thomas Merton can be seen as an exemplary human being, someone attentive to the "monastic" or apophatic depth of existence and intent on cultivating this center to the utmost degree of "purity and awareness." To be sure, this cultivation went through many stages of growth and always involved an intense struggle with obstacles, derailments, and apparent defeats. To this extent, Merton can be compared to the "rebel" as portrayed by Albert Camus, a person not endowed with a precharted roadmap or doctrinaire platform but finding his way in the course of struggle and exploration. This is how folk singer Joan Baez saw him when she visited him in 1967. "He was a rebel," she noted. "And I imagine this man tucked so far away [in a monastery] gave priests, nuns and many other people the courage to take steps they would not otherwise have taken."[1]

This is also how one of his close friends and followers, William Shannon, saw Merton: as "something of a rebel." To be sure, the term here is free of any tinge of aggressiveness or violence; hence Shannon also calls him a "gracious" or "genial sort" of rebel. Basically, for Shannon, what Merton struggled against was a mindless conventionalism, a retreat into settled routines that "no longer nourish the human spirit."[2] No doubt there is something correct about this anticonventionalism; but, as I see it, more is involved or at stake. Basically, what Merton was rebelling against was the immense wasteland, the steadily growing desert of modern life, in the West—that is, the rampant neglect or repression of the constitutive depth dimension of life (what Heidegger called the "oblivion of Being," *Seinsvergessenheit/Seinsverlassenheit*). It was by experiencing this wasteland mindfully, and thus perceiving it *as* a wasteland or desert, that Merton was able to gain a foothold and perspective. It was in this way that he discovered his "monastic" calling, a calling constitutive of his being, and that he entered the Trappist monastery at Gethsemani, near Bardstown, Kentucky (and later the hermitage St. Anne's in Steubenville, Ohio). Ensconced in prayerful solitude, he eventually found a pathway to recovery from the desert of modern life—not merely for himself, but for human beings everywhere. As he wrote regarding the "desert fathers" of the early church: these hermits rebelled against the depravations of their age—and thus paved the way for spiritual renewal. Our age, he added, resembles theirs; but our wasteland is "far more complete." Accordingly, "our danger is far more desperate."[3] In the following I pursue Merton's desert path, honoring both his mindfulness and his social commitment— what I call his "contemplative praxis."

Pathways of Solitude

In narrating Merton's life, Shannon divides the story into two equal parts: the time before he entered the monastery (1915–41) and the years in the monastery (1941–68), with each part lasting exactly twenty-seven years. Although I acknowledge the importance of the division, I find it more appropriate and congenial to view Merton's life as a continuous journey along a path of spiritual learning and growth. The outward markers of his life can be quickly recounted (leaving aside numerous side trips). Born in southern France in 1915, Merton spent much of his early childhood (1916–28) in and around New York and in France. Subsequently his father took him to England, where he eventually attended Oakham Public School in Rutland (1929–32) and then entered Clare College in Cambridge to start his academic career (1933–34). His father having died in 1931 (preceded by his mother in 1921), Merton returned to America and enrolled at Columbia University to study mainly literature (1935–40). While still at Columbia, he was received into the Catholic Church in 1938—a first signal of his awakening religious calling. After a failed attempt to join the Franciscan order, he finally entered the Abbey of Gethsemani in December 1941. He died in December 1968 in Bangkok, Thailand, after attending a conference of Christian monks and nuns.

According to his own accounts and recollections, Merton's early life was disjointed and restless, partly due to the frequent travels of his father. Many years of his childhood and early youth were overshadowed by loneliness and despair, something having to do in part with the early loss of both parents. During his later adolescence, he developed a somewhat dissolute and profligate lifestyle that distantly resembled the youthful escapades of St. Augustine. Throughout his young years, he seemed to be troubled by an acute sense of aimlessness—a sense periodically interrupted by an urgent yearning for meaning and a deeper purpose. At the same time, Merton was clearly a highly gifted and alert young man, a budding scholar and writer. During his time in the New York area (in 1933), he wrote on a summer retreat an early novel titled *The Labyrinth*—a title presumably reflecting some of his own meanderings. At Columbia University he encountered and was able to befriend some outstanding teachers: Daniel Walsh, who introduced him to Western philosophy from Thomas Aquinas to Kant and Hegel, and Mark van Doren, the distinguished professor of English literature. Under the latter's guidance, he wrote a master's thesis on William Blake; his doctoral thesis (not completed) was projected to deal with the poetry of Gerard Manley Hopkins.

One trait that characterized Merton from early on—partly as a result of being orphaned—was his fondness for solitude and quiet retreat. Already during his tender years at Oakham School he would frequently go to the hillside outside of Rutland just to think. As he wrote later: "I liked to go there and think about things by myself. . . . I would walk or sit up there for hours, not waiting for anything or looking for anything or expecting anything, but simply looking out over the wide valley and watching the changes of light across the hills."[4] This fondness certainly facilitated his spiritual journey and his later monastic life. His penchant for solitude and quiet reflection is evident in a number of his well-known writings: from *Seeds of Contemplation* to *New Seeds of Contemplation* to *Life and Holiness* and beyond. *Seeds of Contemplation* was written in response to a student's question regarding the point or meaning of the contemplative life. In his reply, Merton pointed to the "seeds" metaphor in the gospel, noting immediately that these seeds are planted by the spirit at a depth dimension in all human beings, although they do not always reach fruition. As he stated: "The seeds of perfect life are planted in Christians through baptism. But seeds must grow before you reap the harvest. . . . Thus, the *seeds of contemplation* are planted, but often they remain merely dormant."[5] Thus the seeds as the depth dimension of humanity constitute a challenge or provocation that can be heeded and nurtured or else covered over and repressed.

In the sequel to this text, titled *New Seeds of Contemplation*, Merton outlined the meaning and origin of the contemplative life still more clearly and forcefully. "Contemplation," we read there, "is the highest expression of man's intellectual and spiritual life. It is that life itself, fully awake, fully active, fully aware that it is alive." In being fully alive, contemplation also recognizes that life is not self-generated but proceeds from a source that is hidden and enigmatic. What is experienced here is "a vivid realization of the fact that life and being in us proceed from an invisible, transcendent and infinitely abundant source." This source is not epistemically known or rationally comprehended; rather, it derives from what mystics have called a "seeing without seeing" or a "knowing without knowing." What is intimated in these expressions is the fact that the source is not a "thing" among things, an object among objects; thus it eludes all binary subject-object conceptions. In Merton's words: "Contemplation is always beyond our cognitive knowledge, beyond our own light, beyond systems, beyond explanations, beyond discourse, even beyond our own self. To enter into its realm one must in a certain sense die." Approaching the issue from a different angle and in a different register, one might say that contemplation is not so much an intentional endeavor or "project" as a response to a call or summons. What we encounter here, we read, is a "response to a call from Him who has no voice and who, most of all, speaks in the depths of our being: for we ourselves are words of His." Seen in this light, contemplation is above everything else an "echo" or response: "It is a deep resonance in the inmost center of our spirit in which our life loses its separate voice and re-sounds with the majesty and the mercy of the hidden and living One. . . . We ourselves become His echo and His answer."[6]

In reading these lines it is important to guard against a certain temptation: the tendency to construe contemplation as a form of introspection or retreat into the recesses of selfhood. Merton himself did not always guard himself sufficiently against this danger. Thus he wrote at one point that "our real journey in life is interior" and elsewhere coined the motto "Speaking Out for the Inside"—a motto that reverberates in the accounts of many interpreters.[7] What needs to be remembered here is Merton's careful distinction between the self-centered "individual" and the receptive/responsive "person," between the inauthentic self lost in everydayness (what Heidegger called "*das Man*") and authentic ek-static existence. As he writes in *New Seeds of Contemplation*: "The person must be rescued from the individual. The creative and mysterious inner self must be delivered from the wasteful, hedonistic and destructive ego that seeks to cover itself with disguises." The text is eloquent in denouncing the modern Western egocentrism deriving in large part from Descartes. "Nothing," we read, "could be mere alien to contemplation than the *cogito ergo sum* of Descartes. This is the declaration of the alienated being, in exile from his own spiritual depths, compelled to seek comfort in a proof of his own existence." Thus, for Merton, the contemplative is not simply a *cogito*, someone "who lives to sit and think," possibly "with a vacant stare." Differently put, in contemplation the individual is not in the driver's seat, pursuing insight as "an object of calculated ambition." This means that contemplative insight is not something we can obtain "with our practical reason" but rather "the living water of the spirit that we thirst for—like a hunted deer thirsting after a river in the wilderness."[8]

What goes for contemplation also goes for solitude (properly conceived). As Merton insists, solitude is not and can never be "a narcissistic dialogue of the ego with itself"; in reality, such narcissism is only a futile attempt "to establish the finite self as infinite," to make it "independent of all other beings." Solitude hence is not solipsism; its only justification resides in its ability to nurture love for "not only God but also other men." For Merton, solitude and solidarity or communion are not mutually exclusive terms. Just as genuine solitude must be distinguished from mere isolation or aloneness, so communion with others must be differentiated from shallow togetherness (especially in modern mass society): "Mere living in the midst of others does not guarantee that we live in communion with them or even in communication with them. . . . But to live in genuine communion is absolutely necessary for us to remain human." Hence Merton's lapidary advice: "Go into the desert [of solitude] not to escape other human beings but in order to find them in God" [as the source of being].[9] To be sure, even when pursued in communion with others, the life of contemplation and solitude is not free of struggle, tribulation, and even torment. In Merton's words: "Let no one hope to find in contemplation an escape from conflict, anguish or doubt." On the contrary, precisely because of its depth dimension, the contemplative experience "awakens a tragic anguish and opens many questions in the heart like wounds that cannot stop bleeding." In fact, in its existential quest, contemplation is a "trial of fire" in which we are compelled to examine radically all preconceptions, dogmas, or beliefs. Here is a particularly stunning and dramatic passage: "Contemplation is no pain-killer. What a holocaust takes place in this steady burning to ashes of old worn-out words, clichés, slogans, rationalizations! . . . It is a terrible breaking and burning of idols, a purification of the sanctuary, so that no graven thing may occupy the place that God has commanded to be left empty: the center, the existential altar that simply 'is.'"[10]

As can be seen, contemplation—especially monastic contemplation—for Merton was not a comfortable bourgeois retreat but a trial by fire, akin to a consuming prophetic zeal for justice and God's kingdom. In one of his early poems, patterned on the words of Psalm 137, he pictured himself as an exile seeking the land of promise: "May my bones burn and ravens eat my flesh, if I forget thee, contemplation."[11] Although Merton's work occasionally leans toward edification, Shannon at one point captures vividly the prophetic quality of this work, a work devoted wholeheartedly to God-search as an infinite quest. "Living a desert existence on the margins of society," Shannon writes, "gives him a vantage point from which he can take up a critical attitude toward the world, its structures and the values it treasures." The reason that someone like Merton "leaves the world" is not to abandon it but rather "to free himself from its delusions so that he can offer a vision of hope rooted in faith and love." To avoid misunderstanding, Shannon emphasizes that the contemplative's vision is not a blueprint or public platform with which all the world's problems could be solved. As he adds: "The contemplative is not a problem-solver, but a prophet. He or she is the 'troubler of Israel' who prods the consciences of people and directs their minds and hearts to the real issues of human existence. He or she is 'something of a rebel,' but a faithful rebel—faithful to the divine word that is fire in their hearts."[12]

Solitude and Solidarity

As stated before, for Merton monastic solitude—far removed from solipsism—involved the quest both for union with God and (equally important) for communion and solidarity with ordinary people everywhere. Hence, in his case, the "breaking and burning of idols" was intimately linked with the demolition of the "*idola fori*" or public ideologies, that is, with what has come to be known as "ideology-critique." In some accounts, this commitment to solidarity is traced to a certain experience of Merton in March 1958 when he was in

Louisville, Kentucky, on an errand and was suddenly overpowered by an acute sense of community with the people around him. As he himself wrote about this experience: "I was suddenly overwhelmed with the realization that I loved all those people, that they were mine and I theirs. . . . It was like waking up from a dream of separation, of spurious self-isolation in a special world, the world of renunciation and supposed holiness." The experience did not prompt him to abandon his monastic existence because it was precisely his contemplation that had opened his eyes to the interhuman bond: "It is because I am one with people that I owe it to them to be alone, and when I am alone, they are not 'they,' but my own self. They are no strangers!" In terms of practical engagement, the experience put Merton on the path of a prayerful praxis that one may call "letting-be." As he wrote: "It was as if I suddenly saw the secret beauty of their hearts where neither sin nor desire nor self-knowledge can reach, . . . the person that each one is in God's eyes."[13]

Although certainly dramatic, one probably should not exaggerate this experience. After all, a sense of solidarity was present in Merton's work from early on (although it may not have been explicitly foregrounded). A good example is a passage found in his early, justly famous text *The Seven Storey Mountain* (in one of its editions). There, in a powerful statement resonating with the Hebrew prophets, he takes his stand with the poor, the oppressed, and the victimized against the presumptuous rulers and owners of this world. "It is my intention," he states, "to make my entire life a rejection of, a protest against the crimes and injustices of war and political tyranny which threaten to destroy the whole [human] race and the world with it. By my monastic life and vows I am saying NO to all the concentration camps, the aerial bombardments, the staged political trials, the judicial murders, the racial injustice, the economic tyrannies, and the whole socio-economic apparatus which seems geared for nothing but global destruction in spite of all its fair words in favor of peace." In a significant addition to this passage, Merton denounces the pious accomplices of injustice and destruction, the hypocritical members of religious establishments who actually "believe in war, believe in racial injustices, believe in self-righteous and lying forms of tyranny. My life must, then, be a protest against these also and perhaps against them most of all."[14]

Despite its stirring language, readers of *The Seven Storey Mountain* have often tended to concentrate exclusively on the more traditional-monastic meditations in the text. However, the commitment to justice is too strong and recurrent in Merton's writings to be bypassed or missed. For my present purposes, I lift up for attention three important books: *Contemplation in a World of Action*, *Conjectures of a Guilty Bystander*, and *Cold War Letters* (arranging them not in chronological order but along the line of an ethical-existential crescendo). The title of the first book indicates already the basic argument: namely, that contemplation—seen as a deeply humanizing endeavor—takes place inevitably "in the world," which happens to be a "world of action." Hence the contemplative cannot simply abscond from his or her context but has to find a mode of agency that inserts itself in the world without betraying its contemplative calling. As Merton admits, due to some of his early writings he had become "a sort of stereotype of the world-denying contemplative—the man who spurned New York, spat on Chicago, and tromped on Louisville, heading for the woods with Thoreau in one pocket, John of the Cross in another." He immediately proceeds to debunk this stereotype and, in the same breath, debunks a host of traditional binaries such as the division between "secular" and "sacred" and the "old dualisms" of time–eternity, matter–spirit, natural–supernatural. Hence the author of the new text is not "the official voice of Trappist silence, the monk with his hood up and his back to the camera"; he is not "the petulant and uncanonizable modern Jerome who never got over the fact that he could give up beer." Rather, he is simply "the voice of a self-questioning human person who, like all his brothers, struggles to cope with turbulent, mysterious, demanding, exciting, frustrating, confused existence in which almost nothing is really predictable, in which most definitions, explanations and justifications become incredible even before they are uttered."[15]

In the preceding passage, the perceptive reader will surely detect echoes of Heidegger's "being-in-the-world" and also of his notion of a "thrown projection." This means that human beings, including contemplatives, always find themselves in the world, which they try to mold and shape. In Merton's words: "On one hand there is a primitive Christian conception of the world as simply an object of choice.

On the other, there is the obvious fact that the world is something about which there is and can be no choice." Giving a concrete personal example, he adds: "That I should have been born in 1915, that I should be the contemporary of Auschwitz, Hiroshima, Vietnam and the Watts riots are things about which I was not first consulted." Yet these were events in which, he wrote, "I am deeply and personally involved" and to which he had to "respond in a sensitive and caring manner." Against this background, "world" emerges as a very complex phenomenon, both his and not his. It is "not just a physical space" (not a mere "container," in Heidegger's language): "It is a complex of responsibilities and options made out of the loves, the hates, the fears, the joys, the hopes, the greed, the cruelty, the kindness, the faith, the trust, the suspicion of all." Being placed into this kind of cauldron, the contemplative—or the reflective human being—has to find a way to act with some degree of integrity and responsiveness to others, where "responsiveness" means the refusal to manipulate, to dominate, or to reject others (that is, a willingness to "let-be"). Acting in the world and thereby "choosing" it, Merton writes, is thus not an "ego-trip" but the acceptance of "a task and a vocation in the world, in history and in time." Differently put, "acting" here means "to choose to do the work I am capable of doing, in collaboration with my brother/sister, to make the world better, more free, more just, more livable, more *human*."[16]

The difficult encounter of the contemplative person with the busy "world" is also at the heart of *Conjectures of a Guilty Bystander*. As Merton confides in his preface, the material of the text is taken from notebooks he kept during the last decade of his life. The material is "personal and conversational" but not of the "intimate and introspective kind" that one would find in a spiritual journal. What the book hence offers is not pure self-reflection but reflection-in-the-world; its notes add up to "a personal version of the world in the 1960s"— because "what a man truly is can be discovered only through his self-awareness in a living and actual world." As on other occasions, Merton remonstrates against the identification of contemplatives with world-denying hermits, against the conception of monks as "hothouse plants, nursed along in a carefully protected and spiritually overheated life of prayer." What is forgotten here is that contemplative life is "first of all *life*, and life implies openness, growth, development" in a world that is constantly changing. Seen from this perspective, Merton states, the pages of the book are "a testimony of Christian reflection in the mid-twentieth century," a confrontation of twentieth-century questions "in the light of a monastic commitment—which inevitably makes one something of a 'bystander.'"[17]

The questions discussed in the book are numerous; in fact, they cover the whole spectrum of issues thrown up by the age. Here I lift up briefly three: racism, Americanism (of the triumphalist kind), and the spreading social wasteland. As Merton makes clear, racism is basically an offshoot of the Western policy of colonialism, a policy tinged with both paternalism and contempt. The most telling case is that of African colonialism. All colonizers, Merton writes, have been firmly convinced "that we are all benevolent, all brave and self-sacrificing: that we have all *loved* Africa." The pretense has been "that it is our very nature to love Africa, Asia, 'inferior races,' etc. And that if they do not recognize this, it is proof that they are by nature inferior since they cannot appreciate the superior benevolence and culture of the white race." In due course, Africa has become "part of our own [Western] pathological myth, part of our sickness." And not only Africa, but something much closer to home: "the American Negro." After all, "we have offered him everything, but he has rejected it ungratefully." Turning to our own time, Merton pinpoints the core of the race problem as follows: the Negro or Black—and other racial groups as well—is "victimized" by the pathologies inherent in contemporary white civilization, which is incapable of handling them. In order to minimize the latent dangers and potential conflicts, white society has to "project their fears" on some object outside, that is, to find scapegoats. Caught up in this social-pathological syndrome is the Negro or Black person, who, Merton says, "has had the misfortune to make himself, his presence, his own conflicts, his own disruption clearly visible at the precise moment when white society is least prepared to cope with extra hazards." The result has been a hardening of attitudes, a "tightening of resistance," that is, developments rendering the situation unmanageable and explosive.[18]

The issue of racism leads Merton quite naturally into the discussion of a certain kind of Americanism—what he calls the "American myth." The basic tenet of that myth is that America is the promised land or "the earthly paradise." Merton does not deny that "America" constitutes indeed a novel and unusual phenomenon in history. "The discovery of America," he writes, "galvanized and inebriated the Western world." It overturned the worldview of the Middle Ages and convinced "Western man" that society was getting off to "an *entirely new start*," entering a new land "without history," hence "without sin and therefore a paradise." This myth could be maintained intact for a few centuries, so long as there was on open frontier, an "unlimited garden" of Eden. However, with the closing of frontiers, the myth began to crumble: "America gradually became the prisoner of that old curse: the historical memory, the total consciousness of an identity responsible for what had happened, for example, to the Indians." The American Civil War finally destroyed the myth of innocence, first in the South, then in the rest of the country: "Since the Civil War, the whole nation has been 'in sin' [out of Eden] and the sin has been inescapable." Americans have had to realize that they too bear "a mark on the forehead," although they do their best to conceal it: "it might turn out to be the mark of Cain!" Thus there is "paradise lost," but the loss is stubbornly denied or repressed. The denial is nurtured by fear: the dread of losing the high pedestal of superior innocence. "What will we do," Merton asks, "when we finally have to realize that we are locked out of the lone prairie and thrust forth into the world of history along with all the other people in the world: that we are just as much *a part of history as all the rest of them*?" This, he adds, will be "the end of the American myth." We can no longer "lean out from our higher and rarified atmosphere, and point down from the firmament to the men on earth and show them the patterns of our ideal republic."[19]

The critique of the American myth is conjoined in the text with the critique of belligerence and its effects on social life. Americans, Merton notes, are fond of celebrating founding events and documents, like the Boston Tea Party and the Declaration of Independence; but they rarely appreciate their invocation abroad. "Let anyone," he says, "start the equivalent of the Boston Tea Party in Vietnam, in Peru, in Brazil, in Venezuela or elsewhere!" Here is the contrast between the "ideal republic" and the inferior people—a contrast that generates belligerence, which, in turn, undergirds both the propensity for war and the habit and fear of perennial warfare. In Merton's words, the "constant menace of war," as well as the "constant untrustworthy assurance that there will not be war," in their combination create deep anxieties and social pathologies. Looked at closely, the global dangers are certainly real, and there is even "no doubt about our society hanging over the edge of an abyss"; but there is precious little critical examination of the deeper sources or causes; instead there is rampant public manipulation. Compounded by misinformation and manipulation, the dangers of belligerence poison social life, transforming it more and more into a wasteland. Imagine, Merton writes, "that we should be so near, at all times, to such enormous folly and tragedy, and all for the fictions and delusions manufactured by our own greed and our own fear!" The result is disorientation and desolation. "There is a huge sense of desperation," he states, "running through this whole society, with its bombs and its money and its death wish. We are caught in the ambiguities of a colossal sense of failure in the very moment of (seemingly) phenomenal success." Many or most people find that the kind of life everyone dreams of is in fact impossible. Basically, "they cannot face leisure; they cannot handle prosperity."[20]

Merton's critical acumen reaches its highest intensity in the so-called *Cold War Letters*, published posthumously in 2006. (In fact, precisely because of their intensity, the letters were prevented from being published earlier by the "authorities.") The book offers correspondence that Merton carried on with a large number of friends and acquaintances in the world between October 1961 and October 1962—that is, at the height of the Cold War (which today must be called the "first" Cold War, given the upsurge of a "second" installment fifty years later). The letters are the expression of a deeply troubled and anguished soul—anguished chiefly about the seemingly headlong drive toward "hot" war and possibly a nuclear apocalypse. Merton was familiar with literature emerging at the time that talked blithely about a "winnable" nuclear war. Referring to Edward Teller's book *The Legacy of Hiroshima*, he calls it "a systematic piece of amorality which will probably have serious and far-reaching effects." As if to atone for this recklessness, he writes to the mayor of Hiroshima, telling him of his "very great love for

Japan and for its spiritual traditions." Unfortunately, such traditions are shunted away almost everywhere. Here is Merton's description of contemporary politics: "Men should use political instruments in behalf of truth, sanity, and international order. Unfortunately, the blindness and madness of a society that is shaken to its very roots by the storms of passion and greed for power make the effective use of political negotiation impossible." Thus, although perhaps desiring peace, people stumble because of fear and other passions (partly manipulated from above). Hence, in terms of the prospect of cold and hot war, "we are all walking backwards toward a precipice. We know the precipice is there, but we assert we are still going forward; this is because the world in its madness is guided by military men, who are the blindest of the blind." As for himself, Merton adds: "I never cease to face the truth which is symbolized by the names of Hiroshima and Nagasaki."[21]

As on other occasions, in this book Merton offers a critique of Americanism (again the triumphalist kind). Writing to his Pakistani acquaintance Abdul Aziz, Merton confesses that he is often disturbed by "the lack of balance" in this powerful country: "It is technologically very strong, but spiritually superficial and weak. There is much good in the people who are very simple and kind, but there is much potential evil in the irresponsibility of the society which leaves all to the interplay of human appetites, assuming that everything will adjust itself automatically for the good of all. This unfortunately is fatal and may lead to the explosion that will destroy half the world, of which there is serious danger." The malaise in society is compounded and deepened by the recklessness prevailing in high places. "Many of us feel," Merton writes to an English friend, "that 1962 is going to be awfully critical. Humanly speaking, the mentality of this country is about as bad as it could be: utterly sinister, desperate, belligerent, illogical. We will either press the button or become fascists." This outcome is not surprising given the character of the powers that be. For, Merton comments, "the country is in the grip of the business-military complex that lives on the weapons and is dominated by them. We have actually reached the state where our weapons tell us what to do": we are "guided, instructed and nurtured by our destructive machines."[22]

The peril of political recklessness would not have been so grim if it had somehow been balanced by a robust spiritual and moral counterforce; but there is little evidence of that. As Merton complains to a fellow priest: Alas, moral theologians are "very wise" in their pragmatism and their avoidance of commitment to anything but "very safe positions"; but these safe positions suddenly tend to yawn wide open and lead us "right into the depths of hell." So, he asks, how much can one trust ministers who complacently urge the people to go along with "disastrous preparations" that will lead to "the murder of millions of innocent and helpless human beings?" The dilemma is spelled out very forcefully in a letter to Clare Booth Luce in early 1962: "Our sudden, unbalanced top-heavy rush into technological mastery has left us without the spiritual means to face our problems. Or rather, we have thrown the spiritual means away." In fact, "our weapons dictate what to do," and they are "friends of the 'preemptive strike.'" The situation is extremely perilous both politically and spiritually: "We are in an awfully serious hour for Christianity, for our own souls. We are faced with the necessity to be faithful to the Law of Christ and His truth." But this is becoming "harder and harder every day and success seems less and less likely." At this point, responsible people—and especially religious or spiritual people—have to remain "articulate and sane" and speak "wisely" on every occasion. Speaking for himself, Merton adds: "We have to try to some extent to preserve the sanity of this nation, and keep it from going berserk which will be its destruction, and ours, and perhaps also the destruction of Christendom."[23]

Ecumenical and Asian Horizons

In the previously discussed writings, Merton speaks not just as a Catholic monk and not even exclusively as a Christian but as a contemplative pondering the present state of being-in-the-world— remembering the definition of a contemplative as a person willing to plumb the depths of human existence. His *Cold War Letters* are filled with passages testifying to his commitment to a broad, ecumenical kind of spiritual humanism beyond the pale of any sectarianism or provincialism. Thus one letter speaks of "the urgent need for a Christian humanism," stressing the term "humanism" despite the risk of creating "wrong impressions." What is meant by the term, he writes, is a properly spiritual notion of the human being, where "human" denotes an open or ekstatic (or apophatic) disposition, an "epiphany of divine wisdom" linking together "the old paradise and the new paradise, the creation and the new creation." Merton's broad, cross-cultural commitment is perhaps most clearly spelled out in his letter to Abdul Aziz, where he says: "I believe my vocation is essentially that of a pilgrim and an exile in life, that I have no proper place in the world, but that for that reason I am in some sense to be the friend and brother of people everywhere, especially those who are exiles and pilgrims like myself."[24]

Given his ecumenical outlook, it is not surprising that Merton found early in life a fellow-traveler and fellow-pilgrim in the Mahatma Gandhi. The "gentle rebel" quite naturally encountered a kindred outlook in the Indian's ethical rebelliousness and opposition to violent oppression. As Shannon reports, Merton's interest in Gandhi went back to his boyhood at Oakham School, where, in a school debate, he vigorously defended Gandhi's plea for "home rule" (swaraj) and for Britain's departure from India. This interest continued in his monastic years. His notebooks of 1956 are filled with entries on the meaning of Gandhian nonviolence (ahimsa). In 1964 he published an essay titled "Gandhi: The Gentle Revolutionary," and a year later another essay, "Gandhi and the One-Eyed Giant"—which became the introduction to his own edited volume Gandhi and Non-Violence (1965). His introduction and the notes preceding different selections give evidence of Merton's profound grasp of the meaning of Gandhi's work (a grasp exceeding that of many "experts"). The opening lines of the introduction place that work in the cauldron of the meeting of West and East, more specifically of the colonizing West and the colonized East. Borrowing a phrase coined by a Dutch writer, Merton presents the West as a "one-eyed" and powerful giant whose entire energy is concentrated in the eye of logic, of abstract reasoning and the ego cogito. By perfecting this eye, the giant has become the "overseer," the Archimedian summit and controller of the world; what is lost in the bargain is the eye of sensibility, of faith and of love. In Merton's words: "The one-eyed giant has science without wisdom, and he broke upon ancient civilizations which had wisdom without science—a wisdom which transcends and unites, which dwells in body and soul together, and which more by means of myth, rite, and contemplation . . . opens the door to a life in which the individual is not lost in the cosmos and in society but found in them."[25]

Merton thought Gandhi saw himself locked in this cauldron, this cultural tug-of-war. He did not simply reject the West in traditionalist complacency. He initially opened himself resolutely to the West, being educated in England: "He was an alienated Asian whose sole function in life was [or seemed to be] to be perfectly English without being English at all, to prove the superiority of the West by betraying his own heritage." But then something happened. He discovered some "holes" in the giant where the latter betrayed his own "science"; this happened in the experience of racist colonialism in South Africa. Looking for remedies, he found them both in India and the "other" West. "So," Merton comments, "he turned his face and his heart once again to India and saw what was really there. It was through his acquaintance with writers like Tolstoy and Thoreau, and then his reading of the New Testament, that Gandhi rediscovered his own tradition and his Hindu *dharma* (religion, duty)." Thus, what took place was a difficult journey, a "homecoming through otherness" which was creative and transformative. What his experiences with racism and colonialism taught him was that there must be a better way, and spiritual traditions in both India and the West showed him the way: the way of nonviolence (*ahimsa*) and "truth-doing" or "justice-doing" (*satyagraha*). In Merton's words: "One of the great lessons of Gandhi's life remains this: [partly] through the spiritual traditions of the West he re-discovered his Indian heritage and with it his own 'right mind'. And in his fidelity to his own heritage and its spiritual sanity, he was able to show people in the West and the whole world a way to recover their own 'right mind' in their own [transformed] traditions."[26]

As one should note, the phrase "right mind" refers not just to reason or the *cogito*; Gandhi never wanted Indians to become replicas of the one-eyed giant. Rather, the phrase refers to "good sense" and especially the "common sense" of the people. In Merton's words: "The awakening of the Indian mind in Gandhi was not simply the awakening of his owns spirit. . . . It was not just a question of Yoga *asanas*, Vedantic disciplines for his own perfection. No, Gandhi realized that *the people of India were awakening in him*." Thus the large masses who had been mostly silent for thousands of years had now found a voice in him. Moreover, the voice radiated and found echoes far beyond the confines of India: "The message of the Indian spirit, of Indian wisdom, was not for India alone; it was for the entire world. Hence Gandhi's message was valid for India and for himself insofar as it represented *the awakening of a new world*." Thus here is the crux: a new world is awakening and is slowly, patiently, (hopefully) nonviolently, and through *satyagraha* shaking off the shackles imposed by the one-eyed giant. For Merton the mind or spirit that is awakening here is a spirit of "inclusion, not exclusion"; it is "not a mind of hate, of intolerance, of rejection or division" but "a mind of love, understanding, and infinite capaciousness"—that is, a large-souled mind (*mahatma*). For Gandhi, he adds, the liberation of India was "a religious duty" because it was only "a step to the liberation of all humankind from the tyranny of violence in others, but chiefly in ourselves." While violence is basically "wordless," human social life is dependent on language, speech, and dialogue. Hence nonviolence for Gandhi was not just a political method or tactic; rather, it was and is anchored in our humanity. In Merton's words, nonviolence was not simply a "marginal strategy" or private religious feeling: "It belongs to the *very nature of social and political life*, and a society whose politics are habitually violent, inarticulate, and unreasonable is a sub-political and therefore *subhuman* society."[27]

As can be seen, Gandhi's message for India was in fact for humanity at large: it was for the humaneness of humanity. In Merton's eloquent language: "In Gandhi the voice of Asia—not the Asia of the Vedas and Sutras only, but the Asia of the hungry and silent masses—was speaking and still speaks to the whole world with a prophetic message. This message, uttered on dusty Indian roads, remains more meaningful than those specious promises that have come down from the great capitals of the earth."[28] Attentive to this message, Merton extended his spiritual pilgrimage from India to other parts of

(Western and Eastern) Asia. In his 1962 letter to Clare Booth Luce he writes: "Now I am very interested in Muslims, and have contact with some." And in his letter to Abdul Aziz he adds: "On the level of experience, there is much in common between Sufism and Christian mysticism."[29] But we know that, at that time, his attention was increasingly moving toward East Asia, especially toward Buddhism and Taoism. It was in the encounter with these spiritual traditions that Merton was finally able to get rid of the Western "one-eyed" monster with its hurtful divisions and dualisms. As he writes in his *Mystics and Zen Masters*, it is Zen Buddhism (above all) that has managed to escape from the Western subject-object binary. What it offers is "the ontological awareness of pure being beyond subject and object, an immediate grasp of being in its 'suchness' and 'thusness.'" This awareness is neither strictly philosophical nor theological but may be called "purely spiritual." What Buddhist spirituality centrally demolishes is the illness of egocentrism, the incarceration of the spirit in the *ego cogito*. "Zen," Merton states, "is at once liberation from the limitations of the individual ego, and a discovery of one's 'original nature' which is no longer restricted to the empirical self but is in all and above all." Hence "Zen insight is not *our* awareness, but Being's awareness of itself in us."[30]

As we know, Merton's ecumenical outreach was not limited to Buddhism but extended also to other Asian traditions. One of his most delightful and fascinating books is titled *The Way of Chuang Tzu* (containing partly translations from and partly free variations on the Chinese classic). What is truly amazing about some of his texts at the time is that they were written, so to speak, "on dry land"— although he did benefit from the counsel of such eminent masters as D. T. Suzuki, Shin'ichi Hisamatsu, and Kitaro Nishida. It was only in October of 1968 that he finally "took the plunge." With the permission of his monastic superiors, he flew from San Francisco toward Asia with great joy and expectation—in his own words: "with a great sense of destiny, of being at last on my true way after years of waiting and wandering and fooling around."[31] One of his first stops was in Calcutta, India, where he addressed a "Temple of Understanding" meeting organized by worldwide ecumenical leaders. In his *Asian Journal* (which he kept meticulously during the trip) he reports these words as part of his speech: "I think we have now reached a stage of (long-overdue) religious maturity at which it may be possible for someone to remain perfectly faithful to a Christian and Western monastic commitment, and yet to learn in depth from, say, a Buddhist or Hindu discipline and experience." In the context of the same Calcutta meeting, Merton jotted down important rules or guideposts for ecumenical dialogue, for attempts to reach understanding across pronounced differences. As he pointed out, ecumenical communication through words is not enough because words can also foster or aggravate disagreements. Hence communication must yield place to practical communion or communal praxis—a praxis that, although it cannot remove differences, can foster a shared way of life: "The deepest level of communication is not verbal communication but communion. It is beyond words . . . beyond concepts. Not that we discover a new unity; we discover an older unity. My dear brothers [and sisters], we are already one; but we imagine that we are not. And what we have to recover is our original unity. What we have to be is what we are."[32]

In November of that year Merton continued his journey by traveling to Dharamsala for several meetings with the Dalai Lama, whom he found to be a "very solid, energetic, generous and warm person" and who advised him especially to get "a good base in Madhyamika philosophy." From there his trip led Merton to Madras (Chennai) and some nearby Hindu temples, and from there to Colombo and Polonnaruva in Sri Lanka, on to Singapore, and finally to Bangkok, Thailand, where he arrived in early December. Reflecting on the Hindu temples near Chennai and the huge Buddha statues in Polonnaruva, he wrote in his journal: "I don't know when in my life I have ever had such a sense of beauty and spiritual validity running together in one, aesthetic illumination. Surely, with Mahapalipuram and Polonnaruva my Asian pilgrimage has come clear and purified itself. I mean: I know and have seen what I was obscurely looking for. I don't know what else remains but I have now seen and pierced through the surface." On December 10, 1968, exactly twenty-seven years after his entrance into Gethesemani, Merton gave a talk in Bangkok before a group of Christian monks and nuns. The topic of his talk was "Marxism and the Monastic Perspective." In his talk he pointed to a certain affinity between the two perspectives, despite a marked difference deriving from the Marxist reliance on materialism and anthropocentrism:

> The whole purpose of the monastic life is to teach men to live by love. The simple precept is the Augustinian formula of the translation of *cupiditas* into *caritas*, of self-centered love into an outgoing other-centered love.... In Marx you can see some of this same desire to evolve from *cupiditas* to *caritas*, when you see the idea of ... a progress from capitalist greed to communist dedication.... That is precisely what monastic community life has always attempted to realize.... It cannot be done in communism. It *can* be done in a monastery.

On that same afternoon, Merton was killed by an accident (electrocution) in his hotel room.[33]

In that accident a remarkable human being passed away, someone who had illuminated the dark corners of our world and given hope to large numbers of people everywhere. He was a contemplative monastic but also (perhaps because of this fact) a fully human being. William Shannon pays tribute to his humanity. "He was real; he detested phoniness and pretense," Shannon writes. "In him we find an earnest, genuine, no-holds-barred human being struggling like the rest of us, to find meaning, seeking to confront the absurdity that life so often appears to be." Above all, "he knew loneliness, homelessness and alienation." This means: he knew the desert; he knew the wasteland of modern society and the ongoing spoliation of social life and the ecological habitat. But, at the same time, he had inspiration and a vision—a vision that led him not away from the "world" but into steady efforts toward illumination and transformation. In Shannon's words: He was "a prophet who had the insight and the wisdom to see the concerns and the questions that really matter in human life," the life of ordinary people. Monastic life, he believed, is or should be "a sign witnessing to the hope of a better future for those whose freedom has been curtailed or destroyed by the forces of oppression and violence." In Augustinian terms, contemplation should pave the way from *cupiditas* to *caritas*; it should be "a journey from realms of unlikeness (to God) to realms of likeness," a pathway "from Egypt to the Promised Land." As Merton himself noted at the time of his visit to Calcutta: "We are in grave danger of losing a spiritual heritage that has been painfully accumulated by thousands of generations of saints and contemplatives. It is the peculiar office of the 'monk' in the modern world to keep alive the contemplative experience and to keep the way open for modern 'technological man' to recover the integrity of his inner depths"—and thereby the integrity of our humanity.[34]

Chapter Four

Herald of Glad Tidings

Pope Francis as Teacher of Global Politics

The voice of the turtledove ...
—Song of Sol. 2:12

Scriptures, some learned people say, are not so much to be read as to be heard—heard with the outer and the inner ear. For there is a voice or voices clamoring for attention, sometimes voices of anguish, suffering, and grief. Thus the prophet Jeremiah says (Jer. 31:15): "A voice is heard in Ramah, lamentation and bitter weeping. Rachel is weeping for her children; she refuses to be comforted because they are no more." In our world today, such lamentation and weeping can be heard everywhere around the world; all of humanity seems to be engulfed in bitter cries of suffering and torment. The prophet Isaiah writes in a general vein (Isa. 40:8): "A voice says: Cry! And I answered: What shall I cry? All flesh is grass and all its beauty is like the flower of the field." But there are also other voices, other calls or invocations. In the same chapter Isaiah states (40:3): "A voice cries in the wilderness: prepare the way of the Lord, make straight in the desert a highway." And he adds (40:9): "Get up to a high mountain, O Zion, herald of good news; lift up your voice with strength, herald of glad tidings."

In the following pages I want to lift up for attention the voice of a contemporary that speaks to us in many modalities or registers: the modes of lamentation, anguish, and grief but also the modes of joy, happiness, and glad tidings. In September of 2014, Pope Francis visited the memorial and cemetery in Redipuglia, Italy, containing the graves of thousands of soldiers from World War I. At that time he said, grief-stricken: "War is madness. . . . War destroys. It ruins also the most beautiful work of God's hands: human beings." Moreover, his lamentation was not confined to the war waged a hundred years ago but extended to our global situation today: "Even today, after the disaster of the Second World War, perhaps one can speak already of a third war: one fought piecemeal, with crimes, massacres, wanton destruction." In the face of this grim scenario, Francis urged humanity to step back from the brink of global abyss and undergo a radical turning or "*metanoia*": "I ask each of you, indeed all of you, to have a conversion of heart: to move from indifference to tears."[1] For Francis—as for any genuine religious leader—such a turn was the precondition for any personal, social, and political renewal, that is, for the proclamation of "glad tidings" or the "joy of the gospel" (to use the title of a book published by Francis in 2013).[2] The confluence of different registers of speech is a main concern of my reflections here.

A Culture of War and Waste (Kaddish)

From the pope's perspective, our contemporary world is by no means a seedbed of glad tidings; on the contrary, our global situation is filled to the brim with bad news, cries of anguish, suffering, and desolation. In his speech at the cemetery in Redipuglia, Francis pointedly said: "Here lie many victims. Today we remember them all. There are tears, there is sadness, there is pain. . . . Humanity needs to weep, and this is the time to weep." His speech, however, reflected not only sadness but also outrage and revulsion regarding the sources or origins of devastation: "Greed, intolerance, the lust for power . . . these motives underlie the decision to go to war, and they are often justified by an ideology; but first there is the distorted passion or impulse." Becoming steadily more pointed and urgent, he added: "In today's world, behind the scenes, there are interests, geopolitical strategies, lust for money and power, and there is the endless manufacture and sale of arms."[3] Certainly a grim picture, and a grim denunciation of motivations running berserk or out of control.

Close attention to the afflictions and miseries of our world is not limited to the pope's memorial homily but pervades all his writings, sermons, and teachings. *The Joy of the Gospel* devotes a central chapter to a discussion of the "crises" and "challenges" of today's world. As Francis writes: "A number of diseases are spreading." Despite the epochal changes set in motion by the "enormous advances" in the sciences and technology, "the hearts of many people are gripped by fear and desperation, even in the so-called rich countries." Almost everywhere, "lack of respect for others and violence" are on the rise, and inequality is patently evident. The pontiff immediately zeroes in on the main source of inequality: the enormous gap between the rich and the poor, the powerful and the powerless. Just as the commandment "Thou shalt not kill" seeks to safeguard human life, he writes, today we also have to say "Thou shalt not" to an economy of exclusion and inequality—because the latter also "kills." While food is being thrown away in large quantities in rich countries, many people are starving; while wealth is concentrated increasingly in the hands of small elites, masses of people are penniless. Under the reigning ideology of "competition and survival of the fittest," the rich and powerful "feed upon the powerless." In Francis's account, we live increasingly in a "throwaway culture" in which human beings are themselves considered consumer goods "to be used and then discarded." The upshot is that the "underside" of society no longer refers simply to the exploited or the disenfranchised but also to "the outcasts, the 'leftovers.'"[4]

The pontiff in his text does not hesitate to challenge the doctrines or dogmas of contemporary economic "science," especially the ideology of neoliberalism. "Some people," he observes, "continue to defend trickle-down theories which assume that economic growth, encouraged by a free market, will inevitably succeed in bringing about greater justice and inclusiveness in the world." For Francis, this opinion—which "has never been confirmed by the facts"—expresses "a crude and naïve trust in the goodness of those wielding economic power"; meanwhile, "the excluded are still waiting." From this angle, the ongoing globalization of markets is by no means an unqualified boon; on the contrary, it sustains a lifestyle of affluence that excludes others, thus ushering in a "globalization of indifference." Under the impact of this indifference, human sensibilities are stunted; we more and more end up "being incapable of feeling compassion at the outcry of the poor, weeping for other people's pain, and feeling a need to help them." Ultimately, the defects of the reigning neoliberal culture can be traced to a glaring human and theological derailment, the emergence of a new "idolatry": "We have created new idols. The worship of the ancient golden calf has returned in a new and ruthless guise in the idolatry of money and the dictatorship of an impersonal economy lacking a truly human purpose."[5]

The reigning ideology, however, is damaging not only materially and religiously but also politically and ethically. The worship of money robs public life of its basic purpose: the effort to cultivate the common good by providing for the just or equitable distribution of resources and life chances. In the pontiff's words, neoliberalism undermines the role of states or governments, which are "charged with vigilance for the common good," to exercise any kind of public leverage. In this way a new, private-economic "tyranny" is born—invisible and often behind the scenes—that "unilaterally and relentlessly" imposes its own laws or rules without accountability to anyone. (One thinks here of private armies, private militias, and privatized prison systems.) To all this we can add—the pontiff continues—"widespread corruption and self-serving tax evasion," which today have taken on worldwide dimensions, showing that "the thirst for power and possessions knows no limits." Allied with this public malaise is the "rejection of ethics," where "ethics" means concern for the welfare of fellow-beings, an outlook that is a precondition for "a more humane social order." In our time, such an ethics is felt to be a "threat" because it condemns the manipulation and debasement of fellow beings. Unfortunately, this debasement is furthered or aggravated by the media, which are often controlled by elites and are satisfied with providing shallow drivel or entertainment: "We are living in an information-driven society which bombards us indiscriminately with data and which leads to remarkable superficiality in the area of moral discernment."[6]

The pope's anguish and dismay about the condition of our world are eloquently stated in *The Joy of the Gospel*, but they are not confined to its pages. During the first two years of his pontificate Francis presented a large number of speeches, sermons, or homilies on different occasions—a number of which are collected in his book *The Church of Mercy* (2014). A crucial chapter in that book is titled "Demolishing the Idols." A major idolatry rampant in our time is the worship of military power and violence. In the pontiff's words, what humanity most urgently needs and desires is "a world of harmony and peace"—in ourselves, in our relations with others, and in and between nations. But the situation is precisely the opposite. Due to the lure of selfishness and greed, we are "captivated by the idols of dominion and power," which open the door to violence and bloodshed. The pontiff at this point recalls the story of the "Fall," in which "man" entered into conflict with himself and creation. Later conflict gave rise to fratricide. The pontiff here recalls God's question to Cain: "Where is Abel your brother?" and also the former's reply: "Am I my brother's keeper?" (Gen. 4:9). Francis believes we are all asked this question; but our response must not be Cain's. No, we *are* "our brother's keeper! To be human means to care for one another!" But we have stopped up our ears and silenced our conscience, thus rupturing the initial harmony; and when this happens, the brother who is to be cared for becomes an enemy to be fought and killed. This, Francis adds, is not a matter of coincidence but the stark truth: "We bring about the rebirth of Cain in every act of violence and in every war. All of us!" Today the rebirth of Cain is being globalized: "We have perfected our weapons, our conscience has fallen asleep. . . . As if it were normal, we continue to sow destruction, pain, death! Violence and war lead only to death; they speak of death. Violence and war are the language of death!"[7]

In *The Church of Mercy*, the pope's denunciation of warmongering is closely connected with his attack on rampant profit-seeking, on the idolatry of the new mammon. In a speech addressed to a general audience titled "The Cult of the God of Money," Pope Francis takes aim again at financial profiteering, linking it this time with wasteful consumerism that is giving rise to a "throw-away" mentality or a "culture of waste." Today, he says, men and women are increasingly "sacrificed to the idols of profit and consumption," leading to a "culture of waste" in which not only food but human beings are discarded or thrown away. In stark language, Francis denounces the steady normalization of indifference endemic in modern society: "That some homeless people should freeze to death on the street—this does not make news. By contrast, when the stock market drops ten points in some cities, it constitutes a tragedy. Someone who dies is not news, but lowering income by ten points is a calamity." What incenses the pope most of all is the insensitivity to human suffering: the fact that people tend to be discarded "as if they were trash" and that human life is no longer considered "a primary value to be respected and safeguarded." But the excessive waste of food and natural resources is also an issue of grave concern: "Let us remember that whenever food is thrown out, it is as if it were stolen from the table of the poor, from the hungry!"[8]

From the small venues of his homilies and speeches in the fall of 2015 Pope Francis carried his message to the seats of global power in Washington and New York. On September 24 he addressed a joint session of the two chambers of Congress. At this point he reminded the assembled representatives of their great task and responsibility, both to the nation and to the world. As he said: "You are called to defend and preserve the dignity of your fellow citizens in the tireless and demanding pursuit of the common good, for this is the chief aim of all politics. A political society endures when it seeks, as a vocation, to satisfy common needs by stimulating the growth of all its members." To this extent, legislative activity is always based on "care for the people." In the same speech, however, the pontiff reminded the audience of the dark side of modern society: of the penchant for selfishness, hatred, and violence. He stated, "All of us are quite aware of, and deeply worried by the disturbing social and political situation of the world today." For increasingly our world is "a place of violent conflict, hatred, and brutal atrocities, committed even in the name of God and of religion." We find violent types of extremism, fueled by religious or ideological dogmas, tearing up societies and communities. In addition, sectarian violence is aggravated by economic division, by the gulf between rich and poor, financial elites and the dispossessed. This divide also causes mayhem. "Why," Francis asks, "are deadly weapons being sold to those who plan to inflict untold suffering on individuals and societies? Sadly, the answer is: simply for money, money that is drenched in blood, often innocent blood."[9]

On the day following his speech to Congress, Pope Francis addressed the United Nations General Assembly in New York, shifting his focus from one country to the world at large. In this address the pope congratulated the General Assembly—then celebrating its 70th anniversary—for the advances made since its creation: the development of international law, the enactment of norms regarding human rights, the furthering of humanitarian law, and the resolution of numerous conflicts in many parts of the world. However, he did not neglect the dark background against which these advances are profiled: "All these achievements are lights which help to dispel the darkness of the disorder caused by unrestrained ambitions and collective forms of selfishness." For Francis, global disorder is manifest particularly in widespread social disorganization, political antagonisms, and "the relentless process of exclusion" (of the poor and disadvantaged). In his words, we are experiencing today a "growing and steady social fragmentation which places at risk 'the foundations of social life' and foments 'battles over conflicting interests.'" Such battles easily decay into military confrontations or clashes; but "war is the negation of all rights as well as a dramatic assault on the environment." In particularly blunt and forthright language, the pontiff in his address denounced the frequent use of military power for the sake of externally induced "regime change," that is, for the purpose of expansionist geopolitical agendas: "Hard evidence is not lacking showing the negative effects of military and political interventions not coordinated between members of the international community." If the practice continues unchecked, the pope speculated, the United Nations may soon deteriorate into a Hobbesian world, that is, a gathering of "nations united only by fear and distrust."[10]

Turning Around (Teshuvah)

Pope Francis's complaint about the prevailing global disorder was not meant as a message of despair; on the contrary, it was designed as a spur to active renewal. "One of the more serious temptations which stifles boldness and zeal," he writes in *The Joy of the Gospel*, "is a defeatism which turns us into querulous and disillusioned pessimists, 'sourpusses.' Nobody can go off to battle unless he is fully convinced of victory beforehand." Francis at this point recalls the words of Pope John XXIII (uttered half a century ago): "We feel that we must disagree with those prophets of doom who are always forecasting disaster, as though the end of the world were at hand. In our time, divine Providence is leading us to a new order of human relations which ... are directed to the fulfillment of God's superior and inscrutable designs." In the same context, Francis also recalls a passage in the gospel that is directly relevant to our time: "While painfully aware of our own frailties, we have to march on without giving in, keeping in mind what the Lord said to Saint Paul, 'My grace is sufficient for you, for my power is made perfect in weakness'" (2 Cor. 12:9). This means that Christian struggle is always a cross, but a cross "which is at the same time a victorious banner borne with aggressive tenderness."[11]

What the scripture passage pinpoints is the fact that change or renewal cannot just be a worldly project carried forward with the same arrogant self-assurance that has produced the global disorder in the first place. This means that change has to be preceded and accompanied by an inner spiritual renewal that is the work of meditation, reflection, and prayer. The pontiff is very explicit on this point. Genuine renewal, he states in the same book, is not the same as "a set of tasks dutifully carried out despite one's personal inclinations"; in fact, it cannot possibly succeed unless "the fire of the Spirit" burns in our hearts. Thus what is needed is the cultivation of an "interior space" that can give meaning and direction to action: "Without prolonged moments of adoration, of prayerful encounter with the word, ... our work easily becomes meaningless"; we fall prey to weariness, and "our fervor dies out."[12] The same conviction was also forcefully expressed in his address to the UN General Assembly. Citing an address to the same assembly by Pope Paul VI (in 1965), Francis said: "The hour has come when a pause, a moment of recollection, reflection, even of prayer, is absolutely needed so that we may think back over our common origin, our history, our common destiny. The appeal to the moral conscience of humanity has never been as necessary as it is today." To this he added the final statement also taken from Pope Paul's address: "The edifice of modern civilization has to be built on spiritual principles, for they are the only ones capable not only of supporting it, but of shedding light on it."[13]

To be sure, just as actions without guiding principles are deficient, good intentions without action are of no avail. This is why in his writings and speeches Pope Francis gives equal emphasis to inspired leadership and sound political principles. In his speech to Congress he reminded his audience of the spirited leadership of Moses, who liberated his people from their enslavement in Egypt, led them on their journey to the "promised land," and maintained their unity by means of "just legislation." In the specifically American context, the same kind of leadership was demonstrated by President Abraham Lincoln, who struggled to emancipate the African American population from bondage, and still later by Martin Luther King Jr., who pursued the "dream" of securing for African Americans the full range of civil and political rights. The pontiff's speech to Congress also lifted up for remembrance the work of Dorothy Day, the cofounder of the Catholic Worker Movement, who aimed to relieve all working Americans of the burden of economic inequality and oppression. "Her passion for justice and the cause of the oppressed," he said, "were inspired by the gospel, her faith, and the example of the saints." Tellingly, precisely in order to balance social activism with the need for inner renewal, the pontiff's speech also commemorated the work of Thomas Merton, the Cistercian monk we met in the last chapter, who was and remains a spiritual guide for many people. In Francis's words: "Merton was above all of man of prayer, a thinker who challenged the certitudes of his time and opened new horizons for souls."[14]

In the cases of the cited figures, practical work was always guided by sound ethical and political principles, especially by the Golden Rule and the maxim of justice. In his references to these figures, the pope's speeches and writings differ sharply from much of contemporary "political philosophy," where such notions are widely shunned.

With regard to the Golden Rule, his address to Congress is particularly forthright. "We need to avoid a common temptation today," he stated: "to discard whatever proves troublesome or inconvenient," for example, the "Golden Rule," which says: "Let us treat others with the same passion and compassion with which we want to be treated; let us seek for others the same possibilities which we seek for ourselves; let us help others grow, as we would like to be helped ourselves." Adding a startling implication for both national and global politics, Francis continued: "In a word, if we want security, let us give security; if we want life, let us give life." Along with the invocation of the Golden Rule, the pope's reflections are enriched by the remembrance and affirmation of the conception of justice articulated by Greek and Roman thinkers. As he observed in his remarks to the UN General Assembly: "To give to each his own (*suum cuique tribuere*), to cite the classic definition of justice, means that no human individual or group can consider itself absolute, permitted to bypass the dignity and rights of other individuals or social groupings." This conception clearly puts up a barrier to any striving for unlimited power or domination: "The effective distribution of power (political, economic, military, technological) among a plurality of subjects, and the creation of a juridical system for regulating claims and interests, are one concrete way of limiting power." The implementation of this limit, the pontiff added, requires as one of its essential elements "constant and perpetual will" (*Iustitia est constans et perpetua voluntas ius sum cuique tribuendi*)— which means that our world demands of all leading politicians a commitment to justice "which is effective, practical, and constant."[15]

The principle of justice, insisting on reciprocity and mutual regard, militates against an excessive individualism or self-centeredness, which has become a central creed of the modern and "postmodern" age. In the words of *The Joy of the Gospel*: "The individualism in our . . . era favors a lifestyle which weakens the development and stability of personal relationships and (also) distorts family bonds." As opposed to this creed or tendency, a crucial ethical demand of our time is the willingness "to respect others, to heal wounds, to build bridges, and to 'bear one another's burden' (Gal. 6:2)." An important part of the need for mutual bonding is the rehabilitation of a word that, under the influence of liberalism, has become nearly apocryphal:

the word "solidarity." In Francis's account, the word is "a little worn and at times poorly understood," but it refers "to something more than a few sporadic acts of generosity." Basically, for him "solidarity" implies "the creation of a new mind-set which thinks in terms of community and the priority of the life of all over the appropriation of goods by a few." More specifically, the term denotes "a spontaneous reaction by those who recognize that the social function of property and the universal destination of goods are realities which come before private property." As the pope adds pointedly, the "convictions and habits of solidarity"—once they are put into practice—open the way to "structural transformation" (especially the removal of the structural causes of poverty) and make it possible.[16]

The issue of solidarity is also a major theme of the pope's *Church of Mercy*, figuring there in the titles of two chapters or speeches. As the pontiff fully realizes, invoking the term implies struggling almost against a cultural taboo. "*Solidarity*," he states boldly, is a "word that frightens the developed world. People try to avoid saying it; to them it is almost a bad word. But it is our word!" The term denotes basically the ability of "recognizing and accepting requests for justice and hope, and seeking roads together, real paths that lead to (shared) liberation." Shunning empty rhetoric and stressing concrete work, the pontiff addresses his listeners: "Ask yourself: Do I bend down over someone in difficulty, or am I afraid of getting my hands dirty? Am I closed in on myself and my possessions, or am I aware of those in need of help?" In our contemporary world this question has a global dimension; for everywhere there are "huge numbers of people who are unemployed or underemployed and countless multitudes suffering from hunger." In this situation, solidarity cannot be limited to sporadic almsgiving. Hence, Francis believes there is a need to rethink solidarity no longer as simple philanthropy but as "a global rethinking of the whole system, as a quest for ways to reform it and correct it in a way consistent with the fundamental rights of all human beings." Continuing with emphatic urgency, the pope adds these memorable words: "It is essential to restore to this word *solidarity*, viewed askance by the world of economics, the social citizenships it deserves." It is not an occasional attitude; rather, it is "a social value, and it asks for its citizenship."[17]

As one should note, Pope Francis's stress on solidarity does not at all involve the endorsement of a monolithic, undifferentiated collectivity. In his writings and speeches he always pays close attention to the rich diversity of phenomena, natural and cultural, in the world; repeatedly he speaks of a "healthy pluralism" that "genuinely respects differences and values them as such." Thus the bond of solidarity that he valorizes is not one imposed compulsively from above but rather one that emerges through lateral interaction from the ground up (what is sometimes called "transversalism"). What is not always sufficiently recognized by observers of his papacy is the extent to which Francis upholds and celebrates dialogue (sometimes to the point of evoking "conciliar" memories). His *The Joy of the Gospel* is full of praise for dialogue and reflections on its deeper meaning. As he writes at one point: "Dialogue is much more than the communication of [or the sharing of information about] a truth. It arises from the enjoyment of speaking and it enriches those who express their love for one another through the medium of words." It is an enrichment that does not consist in the accumulation of things but in the deepening of the persons who "share themselves in dialogue." Since dialogue is mediated by the word (or words)—remembering the biblical teaching that "in the beginning was the word" (John 1:1)—it is not only interpersonal but also transpersonal. Thus dialogue involves not just the interlocutors but an "intermediary" who guides and inspires understanding. This is how words can "set hearts on fire."[18]

While honoring the "transpersonal" élan, Pope Francis is emphatic in stressing the broad range of situations in which dialogue is needed today. *The Joy of the Gospel* singles out three main areas in which dialogue can and should promote social justice and peace: first, dialogue with states or governments; second, dialogue among groups in and between societies; and third, ecumenical and interfaith dialogue inside and outside the church. It is in the first category that dialogue is perhaps most urgently required. "I ask God," Francis writes, "to give us more politicians capable of sincere and effective dialogue aimed at healing the deepest roots—and not simply the appearances—of the evils in our world." Of great importance also is intra- and intersocietal dialogue: "I beg the Lord to grant us more politicians who are genuinely disturbed by the state of society, the people, the lives of the poor!" What need to be bridged or reconciled on this level are festering rifts dividing cultural and ethnic communities as well as gulfs separating castes, status groups, and economic classes. Of special concern to the pontiff is the need to cultivate good relations among Christian churches (Catholic, Protestant, Orthodox); he urges them to "put aside all suspicion and mistrust and turn the gaze to what we are all seeking: the radiant peace of God's face." Of equal significance, in our globalizing age, is the need to foster harmony with other world religions as well as with nonbelievers. In this respect, he says, "we hold the Jewish people in special regard because their covenant with God has never been revoked." In *The Joy of the Gospel* the pope also ponders the demands placed on Christian faith by encounters with Islam, Hinduism, and other great religious traditions. On all levels, justice and the common good are the yardstick: "A dialogue which seeks social peace and justice is in itself, beyond all merely practical considerations, an ethical commitment which brings about a new social situation."[19]

Glad Tidings (Tikkun)

The aim of dialogue for Francis, one needs to realize, is not so much the honing of argumentative skills as the opening of new horizons pointing ultimately to a promise. He is forthright in stating this promise: "The new Jerusalem, the holy city (Rev. 21:2–4) is the goal toward which all humanity is moving"—although moving in spurts and past many dead ends and derailments. To bring "glad tidings" is to remember this promise and to prepare the way for making "the kingdom of God present in our world." To be sure, the world is not very hospitable to this kind of preparation. As Francis acknowledges, a desert is growing in our world, producing a "desertification" militating against efforts of renewal. But it is precisely in the desert that people are needed who, by the example of their own lives, "point out the way to the Promised Land and keep hope alive." Precisely in our desert condition, "we are called to be living sources of water from which others can drink." These living sources, Francis adds, are not just for special individuals or select groups but for all people. To this extent, glad tidings have "a clear social content"; at their very heart is "life in community and engagement with others." Citing the *Compendium of the Social Doctrine of the Church*, Francis writes that redemption has a social dimension because God "redeems not only the individual person, but also the social relations existing between persons."[20]

In an important section of *The Joy of the Gospel*, the pope reflects on four major principles that, arising out of existential tensions, facilitate the movement toward social justice and peace. One refers to the tension between openness and limitation, between time and space, infinity and finitude. "People," Francis writes, "live poised between a finite moment and the greater horizon of a utopian future." The tension has to be carefully negotiated by retaining the sense of finitude while tilting the balance toward open potentiality. Another issue is the tension between wholeness and particularity, unity and diversity. The best way to deal with this tension, for Francis, is to face it head-on and to make it "a link in a chain of opening horizons" where differences can be reconciled. A further conundrum is the tension between abstract theory and concrete practice, a tension that can be overcome or at least mitigated only by "putting ideas into practice"; for "not to make them reality, is to build on sand." A final issue, particularly relevant today, is the relation between globalization and localization. "We need to pay attention to the global," Francis writes, "so as to avoid narrowness and banality"; but on the other hand, attention to local problems "keeps our feet on the ground." By navigating a path between these tendencies, we avoid getting caught up in either a top-down universalism or else "a museum of local folklore."[21]

The image of global order that inspires Pope Francis is a complex combination of wholeness and diversity, of centripetal and centrifugal elements. In his words: "Our model is not the sphere, which is no greater than its parts, where every point is equidistant from the center, and there are no differences between them. Instead it is the *polyhedron*, which reflects the convergence of all its parts, each of which preserves its distinctiveness." Differently put, "polyhedron" means "the convergence of peoples who, within the universal order, maintain their own individuality." A very important aspect of the pope's global vision is the fact that it includes not only Catholics, and not even only religious believers, but also people outside any religious affiliation, such as secular humanists, who lead decent and upright lives. "As believers," Francis writes, "we also feel close to those who do not consider themselves part of any religious tradition, yet sincerely seek for years for truth, goodness and beauty." We consider them as "precious allies in the commitment to defending human dignity, in building peaceful coexistence between peoples and in protecting creation." In a surprising and exhilarating passage, the pope refers to the possibility of a global forum (or global forums) bringing together people of good will globally for discussion and cooperation. "A special place of encounter," he writes, "is offered by new Areopagi such as the Court of the Gentiles where 'believers and non-believers are able to engage in dialogue about fundamental issues of ethics, art and science, and about the search for transcendence.'" This, too, he adds, is "a path to peace in our troubled world."[22]

By way of conclusion, let me lift up again the theme that runs through all of Francis's writings and speeches, serving as a kind of *basso continuo*: the theme of bringing good news or glad tidings. As he states at one point, citing Mark and St. Paul, the mandate of all faithful people is to "go into all the world and proclaim the good news to the whole creation" (Mark 16:15), for the creation "waits with eager longing for the revealing of the children of God" (Rom. 8:19). If this mandate is fulfilled or implemented, he adds, "the life of society will be a setting of universal fraternity, justice, peace and dignity."[23] Thus, in the midst of the bad news tormenting humanity on a daily basis, the pontiff holds up a beacon of gladness and redemption—a beacon operating not just in another world or in the afterlife but in our world. "Let us believe scripture," he writes, "when it tells us that the kingdom of God is already present in this world and is growing, here and there, and in different ways . . . like the good seed that grows amid the weeds (Matt. 13:24–30) and can always pleasantly surprise us."[24] In upholding this trust, Pope Francis is like the messenger of whom Isaiah says: "How beautiful upon the mountains are the feet of him who brings good tidings, who publishes peace, who brings good tidings of good, who publishes salvation" (Isa. 52:7). The glad tidings mentioned here are the tidings of "a good land, a land of brooks and water, of fountains and springs, a land of vines, fig trees and pomegranates, of olive trees and honey" (Deut. 8:7–8). This is a place filled with the fragrance of "a rose of Sharon, a lily of the valleys," where "flowers appear on the earth, and the time of singing has come" and where "the voice of the turtledove is heard in our land" (Song of Sol. 2:1, 12).

Chapter Five

Modes of Religious Spirituality

Some Christian and Islamic Legacies

Having discussed, in the preceding chapters, four exemplary recent or contemporary spiritual leaders, the time has come for broader theoretical (philosophical/theological) reflections on the meaning of religious spirituality and its different modes. As I see it, adopting a broader theoretical perspective does not necessarily mean exiting from spiritual engagement to gain a "view from nowhere"; rather, to maintain traction, reflection has to stay close to experience (this is also why real-life mentors are memorialized at the front of this book). Thus in the following observations I aim not to abscond from but rather to move more deeply into the spirituality exemplified in prior chapters. One point that emerges from these chapters is the close connection between (what one may call) "vertical" and "lateral" spirituality, that is, between a spiritual orientation toward divine "transcendence" and one toward fellow human beings, or else between religious faith and concrete praxis. It seems that today, the invocation of God or the divine divorced from any lateral engagement is simply no longer tenable; at the same time, lateral praxis severed from spiritual moorings arouses the suspicion of self-centered manipulation. Paul Tillich spoke in this context of a "kairological moment"—an expression picked up by Panikkar and in different terms by Merton. For Panikkar, the close interpenetration of faith and lateral praxis—captured in the phrase "sacred secularity"—was even a unique temporal event or a "hapax" phenomenon.[1]

As the present chapter shows, the two dimensions have historically tended to be more neatly distinguished—although they were never completely divorced. To make sense of the two dimensions from a historical perspective, I introduce in the following a distinction between two types of spirituality: a "gnostic" or illuminationist type oriented toward unity with God and an *agape*-centered type oriented toward engagement with and service to one's fellow beings. Expressed in linguistic terms, the first type gives preference to monologue (of the believer with God or of God with himself), while the second grants priority to dialogue or conversation. Behind these types emerges, of course, the traditional theological hierarchy of the "two worlds": the this-worldly and the other-worldly, the "secular" and the "sacred" domains. What Panikkar calls the "hapax" phenomenon is the experience that, in our time, the two domains can no longer be neatly separated. This does not mean that they are simply amalgamated or fused; rather, the difference or distinct integrity is maintained in their correlation. The phrase sometimes used by Martin Heidegger, that "Being *is* beings"—where "is" has a transitive status—points precisely to this kind of differentiated correlation (the "ontic-ontological difference"), located beyond theism, atheism, and pantheism.[2]

Apart from delineating two main types of spirituality, the present chapter aims to lend to the topic not only greater historical depth but also (and still more importantly) greater geographical breadth—something surely desirable in our globalizing age. In this respect, our era certainly places numerous question marks behind Rudyard Kipling's famous dictum that "West is West, East is East, and never the twain shall meet."[3] Perhaps, in Kipling's time, the statement still had a ring of truth. When, in 1893, the great Indian Swami Vivekananda visited the Parliament of the World's Religions in Chicago, he reportedly told a journalist inquiring about his impressions: "I bring you spirit, you give me cash." His response reflected a prevailing sentiment at the time about a deep cultural divide according to which Western culture was synonymous with materialism, while the East resonated with spirit or spirituality. Even if it was perhaps plausible at that time, the division no longer prevails today (at least in this crude form). When, a hundred years after Vivekananda's visit, another meeting of the Parliament of the World's Religions was held in Chicago in 1993, the delegates—numbering nearly seven thousand—pledged themselves to work for a worldwide "transformation in individual and collective consciousness," for "the awakening of our spiritual powers through reflection, meditation, or positive thinking"—in sum, for "a conversion of the heart." In the words of the keynote speaker, Robert Muller (a former deputy secretary general of the United Nations), the aim was to build "a world cathedral of spirituality and religiosity."[4]

As we know, of course, from hindsight, the noble goal was not achieved—maybe in part because of the relative sidelining of the "lateral" or practical side of spirituality (in favor of *gnosis*). In an effort to guard against this sidelining—and also against the opposite danger of a facile absorption of spirituality into consumer culture—this chapter first of all reflects on the meaning of religious "spirituality" as it has been handed down by a number of religious traditions. Seen from the vantage point of these traditions, spirituality is not (certainly not principally) a form of individual faculty or psychic subjectivism; rather, it more precisely involves a mode of self-transgression: an effort to rupture narcissism or self-centeredness by opening the self toward "otherness" (which is variously described as God, as cosmos or the world-soul, or as other human beings). For the sake of brevity, my discussion focuses chiefly on the traditions of Christianity and Islam—although I offer some side glances at other spiritual legacies. Within the confines of these traditions, I invoke the distinction between spiritual types (previously mentioned)—in full recognition of the fact that the typology inevitably shortchanges the rich profusion of spiritual life over the centuries. Following some broad theoretical reflections, my presentation exemplifies these reflections by turning to a number of prominent spiritual leaders or guides. Returning to the contemporary situation, the concluding section asks which mode or modes of spirituality may be most fruitful and commendable in our present, globalizing context.

The Traditional Meaning of Spirituality

As the word indicates, "spirituality" derives from "spirit" and hence designates (or is meant to designate) some manifestation of the work of spirit. Most of the great world religions have terms that are akin to "spirit" or capture some aspect of it. Thus we find in the Hebrew Bible the term *ruach*, in the Arabic of the Qur'an *ruh*, in the Greek version of the New Testament the word *pneuma* (and/or *logos*), translated in the Latin Vulgate as *spiritus*—and the list could probably be expanded to include the Sanskrit *brahman* and the East Asian *tao*. Unfortunately, this concordance or parallelism of terms does not yet offer clues for unraveling their meanings. All the words mentioned are inherently ambivalent and open to diverse readings. Thus, to take the nearest example, the English "spirit" is closely related to "spirited," "spiritistic," and even to "spirit" in the sense of an alcoholic beverage; in turn, the French equivalent, *esprit*, conjures up other connotations (of wittiness, intellectual cleverness, or virtuosity)—not to mention the profusion of meanings associated with the German *Geist*.[5] How can we make headway in this multivocity? Here it is good to remember the core feature of religion and/or spiritual experience: the transgression from self to other, from "immanence" to (some kind of) "transcendence." When viewed from this properly religious angle, "spirit" and "spirituality" must somehow participate in this transgressive or transformative movement; differently put, they must be seen as bridges or—better still—as vehicles or vessels suited for navigating the transgressive journey.

Descending from the level of metaphor, it should be clear that spirit and spirituality cannot simply be equated with or reduced to a human "faculty," as the latter term has been understood in traditional anthropology and psychology. Traditional teachings about "human nature" commonly distinguish between at least three main faculties or attributes: the faculties of reason (or mind), will (or willpower), and emotion or sensation (a tripartition reflected, for example, in the Platonic division of the human psyche into *nous*, *thymos*, and appetite). While reason enables us to "know," will—in this scheme—enables us to "act" and emotion or sensation to "feel."[6] Located squarely in human "nature," none of these faculties can be directly identified with spirit or spirituality—although none of them should be construed as its simple negation or antithesis. Thus, without being antirational or irrational, religious spirit cannot be equated with human rationality—because it is the work or breath of the spirit that allows reason to reason and to know anything in the first place. Likewise, spirit cannot be collapsed into will for the simple reason that divine grace and transformation cannot merely be willed or unwilled (although it may require a certain human willingness or readiness). Finally, spirit cannot or should not be leveled into sentimentality or emotionalism—despite the fact that it cannot operate without engaging human sentiment or feeling in some way. It is in order to guard against such equations that religious traditions typically insist on terminological distinctions. Thus the Hebrew *ruach* is set over against *binah* (rational mind) and *nephesh* (organic life); the Arabic *ruh* over against *'aql* (reason or intellect) and *nafs* (desire); the Greek *pneuma* over against *nous* and *thymos*; the Latin *spiritus* over against *ratio* and *voluntas*. None of these distinctions—it is important to note—should be taken in the sense that spirit is elevated into a kind of super- or hyper-faculty: far from being another, though higher, property or attribute, spirit basically supervenes and unsettles all properties by virtue of its transformative-transgressive potency.

What this means is that spirit not only resists terminological univocity; it also disturbs ontological and anthropological categories. As a transgressive agency, spirit addresses and transfuses not only this or that faculty but the entire human being, body and mind, from the ground up. In traditional language, the core of the "entire human being" tends to be located in the "heart" or the "soul" (corresponding to the Chinese *hsin*, meaning "heart-and-mind")—provided these terms are not in turn substantialized or erected into stable properties. To this extent, one might say that spirit and spirituality are, first of all, affairs of the heart (or heart-and-mind).[7] This means that, without being an attribute or faculty, spirit also cannot be defined as a purely external or heteronomous impulse; rather, to perform its work, it necessarily has to find a resonance or responsiveness "inside" human beings—which is the reason that spirituality, quite legitimately, is commonly associated with a certain kind of human "inwardness." (This insight is one motivation behind Tillich's distinction between heteronomy, autonomy, and theonomy and Panikkar's distinction between heteronomy, autonomy, and ontonomy.) Looking at the development of religious traditions, one can probably say that religious history shows a steady deepening and also a growing complexity of inwardness.

Thus, during the early phases of Christianity, spirituality was closely linked with doctrinal theology, which, in turn, was mainly the province of a clerical or ecclesiastic elite. Church historians speak in this context of a "spiritual" or "mystical theology," linking this term with such names as Pseudo-Dionysius and Jerome and, later, Bernard of Clairvaux and St. Bonaventure.[8] In many ways, the Reformation brought an intensification and also a growing popular dissemination of spirituality. Martin Luther, for example, differentiated between an "external" and an "inner" man (or human being) and clearly associated spirit—chiefly the Holy Spirit—with human inwardness.[9] At the same time, the Reformation released spirituality from its earlier clerical confinement (in accordance with the idea of the "priesthood of all believers"). Still more recently, partly as a result of Romanticism and progressivism, spirituality has been further democratized. Leaving aside fashionable forms of contemporary spiritualism (criticized in the preface), Charles Taylor is surely correct when he states that religion cannot simply be an external form or constraint but has to find some kind of personal "resonance" among people today.[10] Viewed from this angle, the heart (or heart-and-mind) might be described as the great "resonance chamber" constantly open or attuned to new religious or mystical experiences (in a mode of fine-tuning or "high fidelity").

To be sure, to perform its task this resonance chamber cannot be self-contained or resonate only within itself but must remain attentive to an address or supervening appeal. Here we need to return to the central point of spirituality: its role as a great vessel (or *mahayana*) navigating the straits between immanence and transcendence, between the human and the divine.[11] Obviously there are different ways of navigating these straits; in fact, the history of religions reveals a great variety of pathways. To grasp their difference, one needs to recall again the "in-between" character of spirituality, its placement between the two shores of worldly finitude and infinity. Basically, one can interpret the image of the "two shores" in two different and even opposite ways. One can construe their relation as starkly hierarchical or vertical; in this construal, the divine shore (so to speak) differs from the worldly in the same manner as higher relates to lower or as light stands over against darkness, spirit against matter. On the other hand, one can construe the two shores as more analogous and laterally differentiated; in this case, the finite and infinity are linked in the mode not of negation or strict subordination but of sublimation and transformative analogy. As one should note, both varieties affirm a kind of distinction or difference. But in the first case, the distinction is radical and ontological, while in the second case it is mediated, dialectical, and dialogical. (Tillich's notion of "dialectical theology" can be seen in this light.)

The idea of spiritual hierarchy—combined with the insistence on absolute divine supremacy—is chiefly linked with the traditional teachings of "gnosticism" (or at least prominent strands in gnosticism).[12] Most of the great world religions evince traces of gnostic beliefs; however, as a full-fledged doctrine, gnosticism seems to be a specialty of the Middle East or of West and South Asia. As is well known, a major example of gnostic spirituality was Manicheism, which can be traced to the Babylonian sage/prophet Mani. But its origins seem to be much older and go back to ancient Middle Eastern and Persian forms of light worship. During the Hellenistic period, older types of gnosticism became fused or infused with elements of Neoplatonism as well as with Jewish and Christian forms of "*logos-mysticism.*" A basic assumption in traditional gnosticism is the notion of an initial division or contraction in the divine or the godhead, a division that became manifest with the creation of the outer world, a creation ascribed to a "demiurge." Since the time of this creation, a basic duality (or "dyotheism") has operated: the distinction between the hidden, unknown, and nonmanifest God and the overt, knowable, and manifest world. Hellenistic gnostic texts described God variously as the "Great Absence," the "Supreme Void," or the "Abyss" (*Bythos*)—a void covered over by the manifest world (the creation of the demiurge) and into which that world eventually needs to be "emptied." Corresponding to this cosmic duality is a division of modes of knowledge: although the manifest or external world can be known "exoterically" by everybody, knowledge of the godhead is necessarily "esoteric" and is reserved in stages only to the select few endowed with the divine spark or spirit—a feature that tends to lend to gnostic movements a secretive or hermetic character. The supreme aim of gnostic knowledge is complete fusion or unity with the divine, which means that an initial duality is replaced by monism.[13]

It is chiefly on this point that *agape* or service-oriented spirituality demurs. By not accepting the radical dualistic scenario, *agape* spirituality also refuses to endorse its telos or cosmic teleology. In lieu of the eventual conquest or erasure of the world by the divine, *agape* stresses the mediated and "covenantal" relation between the two shores; accordingly, the gnostic path of "deification" or self-deification is here replaced by the ascending path of loving redemption, a path that frequently or commonly implies service to one's fellow beings. Here the linguistic distinction previously invoked returns. Whereas the gnostic path is monological and ultimately monistic, the *agape* path is dialogical and redemptive.[14]

This may be an opportune moment to take a brief glance at spiritual traditions outside the range of the so-called Abrahamic religions. In the Indian tradition, the previously stated distinction between spiritualities corresponds closely to the distinction of spiritual paths or *yogas* delineated in the *Bhagavad Gita*. Thus the type of gnostic spirituality finds its parallel in *jñana* yoga or the path of intellectual wisdom of which the *Gita* says (4:33) that "greater than any work or earthly sacrifice is the sacrifice of sacred wisdom. For wisdom is in truth the end of all holy work." On the other hand, *agape* and service spirituality are reflected in the yogas of *bhakti* (devotion) and *karma* (action), which are celebrated together in these lines (3:30–31): "Offer to me all thy works and, free from vain hopes and desires, rest thy mind in the Supreme. Those who thus follow my yoga and have devotion/faith and good will, find through pure work their freedom." In this context, one might also remember that classical Indian philosophy, especially the branch of "Vedanta," has centrally revolved around the issue of whether ultimate "Being" is essentially one (monism) or two (dualism) or something in between. To some extent, the previously mentioned Indian yogas are still preserved in Mahayana Buddhism, especially in the combination of the practice of meditation or contemplation (especially in Zen Buddhism) and the celebration of devotion (in Shin Buddhism) and liberating practice and compassion (*karuna*, as exemplified by Bhodisattvas).

Christian Spiritualities

Throughout its history, Christianity has provided fertile ground for many kinds of spirituality.[15] To be sure, relations with the official church (or churches) have always been uneasy or tense, frequently giving rise to oppression or persecution. As a form of personal religious resonance, spirituality by its nature tends to be suspect in the eyes of scriptural literalists and clerical traditionalists. Suspicion and hostility overshadowed the lives of most of the illustrious medieval and early modern mystics. Thus the great mystic and Dominican preacher Meister Eckhart (1260–1328) was accused of heresy by Rome and subjected to Inquisition proceedings, first in Cologne and later in Avignon (then the site of the papal residence); after his death a large number of his views were condemned as heretical. Likewise, the Spanish Carmelite mystic John of the Cross (1542–91) was harassed by the higher clergy and finally imprisoned in a cloister, just as at an earlier time Mechtilde of Magdeburg (1207–82) had been hounded by the same clergy whom she criticized for their worldly ambitions. Even such a relatively orthodox thinker as Ignatius of Loyola (1491–1556) was interrogated by the Inquisition and accused of being a member of the "Alumbrados" (a sect of "free thinkers"). Tensional relations continued after the Reformation and gave rise to recriminations between orthodox Lutherans and Calvinists, on the one side, and pietists, free sects, and "*Schwärmer*" (enthusiasts), on the other. Still more recently, recriminations took on a confessional or denominational slant. Thus the Protestant theologian Adolf von Harnack denounced mystical spirituality as a typical outgrowth of Catholic faith; intensifying the invective, the Swiss Emil Brunner wrote even more pointedly: "Christian mysticism is a blending of faith and mystification, of Christianity and paganism—a blending which characterizes Catholicism as a whole."[16]

Leaving aside surface skirmishes or polemics, it seems advisable to return to the two main types of spirituality mentioned before. Of the two types, gnostic spirituality has undoubtedly suffered the most severely at the hands of official Christianity (or "Christendom"). Although there have been many motives, the hostility has chiefly been due to official views regarding the centrality of Jesus as the Christ and redeemer—a centrality that is likely to be sidelined by an emphasis on esoteric illumination. This does not mean that there has been an absence of gnostic strands in Christianity. As one will recall, early Christianity emerged in the context of late Roman and Hellenistic civilization, which, in many ways, was a vast "spiritual marketplace" that brought together a multitude of traditions and beliefs; one of the prominent currents was gnosticism. As historians have shown, the very birth of Christianity was attended, and even assisted, by a host of sectarian movements (inside and outside of Judaism) with gnostic or semignostic leanings. Students of the period are familiar with the "Merkaba" mystics of Palestinian Judaism, with the teachings of the Essenes (known through the Dead Sea scrolls), and with the Nag Hammadi documents discovered in upper Egypt (in 1940). These and other findings give evidence of a broad "illuminationist" ferment gripping the Middle East at the time. Surrounded by this ferment, the early Christian church was the arena of intense struggles dedicated to distinguishing official from unofficial or heretical beliefs. Sometimes gnostic views were propounded by reputable church leaders, such as Basilides in the East and Valentinus and Marcion in the West.[17] Slowly solidifying their doctrinal position, the early church fathers—led by Irenaeus and Tertullian—launched a concerted offensive against heretics and successfully expunged or marginalized gnostic spirituality (Marcion and Valentinus were excommunicated around AD 150).

This, of course, was not the end of Christian gnosticism. During the Middle Ages and early modernity, many new gnostic or semignostic movements arose in Western and Eastern Christianity. Students of history recall such names as Catharism and Bogomilism and also such sects as the Albigensians, Waldenses, and Alumbrados. Links with gnostic teachings can also be detected in the spirituality of the Knights Templar (Knights of the Temple of Solomon) and of the Rosicrucians—movements that in later centuries were succeeded by Masonic lodges and, still more recently, by the networks of theosophy and anthroposophy. It was chiefly in the fight against medieval and early modern gnostic sects that the Inquisition gained its reputation of religious intolerance. During the thirteenth century, larger-scale crusades were mounted by the church against heretical sects, in the course of which large numbers of Cathars, Albigensians, and others were massacred. Often the church could rely on the complicity of temporal rulers, especially in France. Thus, during the reign of Philip le Bel (1268–1314), Jacques de Molay, grand master of the Templars, and thousands of other Templars were arrested throughout France (on Friday, October 13, 1307). A few years later, the grand master and another leading Templar figure were publicly burned on a slow fire as heretics.[18] In this respect, the Protestant Reformation signaled an end of large-scale physical persecution but not an end of polemical invective. It was against the semignostic spirituality of the *"Schwärmer"* (enthusiasts) that Luther's student Zinzendorf uttered his scathing words of condemnation (which probably should not be extended to Christian spirituality as such). Such spirituality, he stated harshly, leads to "arrogant conceit" (*Einbildung von sich selbst*) and "self-righteousness" without Christ, and hence to a form of human "self-deification" that is "a dangerous and miserable doctrine opposed to the very core of creation."[19]

Although generally hostile to gnostic teachings, Christianity has always been relatively hospitable to erotic mysticism or *agape* spirituality. Notwithstanding his strong denunciation of the *Schwärmer*, Martin Luther himself repeatedly resorted to erotic symbolism to portray the relation between Jesus and Christian inwardness: namely, the image of bridegroom and bride. This symbolism, of course, is much older than Luther and throughout the Middle Ages served as a vehicle for expressing the relation between Jesus and the community of believers.[20] In Christian *agape* spirituality, the loving relation between bridegroom and bride is first initiated by Jesus and only then reciprocated by human beings. As we read already in St. Paul's letter to the Galatians (2:20): "I live by faith in the son of God who loved me and has given Himself for me." A similar sentiment is expressed in the fourteenth-century text *Imitatio Christi*, which states: "If you rely on yourself alone, nothing is accomplished; but if you rely on God, heaven's grace redeems you."[21] In every case, Christian *agape* involves a loving relationship between an "I" and a "You" or "Thou," between humans and fellow humans and humans and the divine. And like every genuine love, this relationship is basically ambivalent and cannot be captured either in a rigidly dualistic or else a synthetic or monistic formula. "I and You" here implies a two-ness or duality (or difference) that can be mediated or bridged through love but cannot be abolished either through appropriation of the "other" by the self or through the dissolution of the self in the "other." As Gerhard Ebeling has correctly noted: "Even in the most intimate union with Christ a difference remains. For although genuine love unites, it does not cancel duality in an indiscriminate fusion devoid of language and communication."[22]

These comments can be illustrated by a brief glance at prominent Christian *agape* mystics. Thus the "spiritual poetry" of John of the Cross (1541–91) is in essence a series of love songs exploring the depth and ecstasy of the human encounter with the divine. As he states in one of these songs:

> Oblivious of created things,
> recollecting the Creator alone,
> the depths of inwardness we plumb,
> by loving lovingly the Beloved.

"Plumbing inwardness," one should note, signifies here neither a retreat into solipsism nor a gnostic-intellectual union with the divine. As John himself elaborates: "Our soul becomes unified with God not through cognition or mental representations, nor through passive enjoyment or anything sensual, but intellectually only through faith, recollectively through hope, and actively through love"—where love means an ek-static movement toward the "You" of God and also laterally toward the "You" of fellow human beings; again in John's words, with love of God "love for fellow beings likewise grows."[23] A similar orientation is manifest in John's compatriot, Teresa of Avila (1509–82). In Teresa's case, love of God means love for the crucified Jesus—which translates concretely into loving care for the needy and the suffering of humankind. As it happens, this linkage or translation was not present from the beginning. In fact, during her early monastic life, Teresa was strongly attracted to a kind of superspiritual (and quasi-gnostic) union with the divine that was disdainful of worldly concerns. However, in 1554 a religious experience of the "mortally wounded Jesus" changed her outlook. The impact of this experience is recorded in her autobiography, where she writes that, under the influence of certain spiritual teachers, she had initially believed

> that everything bodily [or worldly] was only an obstacle to complete contemplation which is a purely spiritual exercise. . . . God willing, this [contemplative] mode of prayer is indeed very tasty and pleasurable. . . . Hence, nobody could have prompted me to return to a consideration of the humanity of Jesus which appeared to me then as a mere distraction. . . . Had I remained in this stance, I would never have reached my present position; for I now consider that [earlier] stance an error. . . . Lord of my soul and my highest good: crucified Jesus! I never remember without pain my earlier delusion which now appears to me as a great betrayal of you.[24]

Examples of this kind could be multiplied; for our present purposes, however, a few additional illustrations must suffice. As indicated, for Christians—whether Catholic or Protestant—*agape* spirituality is centered on the encounter with Jesus, and in light of Jesus's suffering and death, this love relation spills over into a loving engagement with fellow humans and their sufferings. For the Dominican Johannes Tauler (fourteenth century), love involved a radical transformation (or *periagoge*), a move through self-denial and mortification to a rebirth effected by Christ's love. This rebirth in and through Christ, however, could not lead to a complete fusion—which would negate human humility and longing. Rather, abandonment of selfish attachments freed the heart for the *imitatio Christi* and for co-suffering with Jesus and the world (the mystical "*compassio*" taught earlier by Bernard of Clairvaux). As Josef Zapf concisely formulates Tauler's teaching: "Abandon self-centeredness and be guided by the life and suffering of Christ. . . . Ponder God's will and your own nothingness. . . . Then God works in all your works and deeds."[25] In a similar vein, the Pietist Count Zinzendorf (1700–60) emphasized the need to anchor Christian spirituality in the life and suffering of Jesus. After an initial flirtation with mystical enthusiasm, Zinzendorf

returned to the more sober Lutheran conception of Jesus as bridegroom and to the redemptive quality of his suffering. As he wrote
at one point: "If there is a genuine mystic, it is Jesus. For a mystic is
someone who lives a hidden life ... which one might call a *statum
mortis*, away from the praise and vituperation of this world."[26]

Before proceeding, a few additional comments seem in order.
An important point to note is that the distinction between gnostic
and *agape* spirituality is not and has never been watertight. Occasionally the two kinds are mingled or interpenetrating—although, on
the whole, *agape* tends to prevail. A case in point is the writings and
teachings of Meister Eckhart. What might be considered gnostic or
semignostic features in Eckhart's work have to do mainly with his
notion of a hidden "godhead" beyond or beneath the personal God,
a godhead variously described as "Being" or "beyond Being" or else
as "Emptiness" and "Abyss"; closely linked with this notion is the
emphasis on an intellectual plunge, a self-emptying submergence of
the intellect in the divine abyss.[27] Although prominent, these features
probably should not be taken in isolation or as a denial of practical
agape. What one can hardly forget is that Eckhart was also a Dominican cleric and as such deeply involved in preaching and pastoral care.
Some of his finest insights are to be found in his Latin and German
sermons. Thus his famous sermon *"Beati pauperes spiritu"* calls into
question precisely the gnostic ambition to "know" and fully plumb
God's mystery through our rational intellect or "spirit"; at the same
time, it questions our ability to reach God through willpower and
mental exercises—counseling instead a "releasement" that will allow
God to work in and through us. It is in this sense that one should probably also understand Eckhart's celebrated sermon on the respective
merits of contemplation versus active life—or, biblically expressed,
the respective merits of Mary and Martha (Luke 10:38–42).[28]

The other Christian mystic frequently associated with gnostic
spirituality is the Silesian Johannes Scheffler, who wrote under the
name of Angelus Silesius (1624–77). In his long and meditative essay
titled *Sauf le Nom*, Jacques Derrida devotes considerable attention to
Scheffler's work, emphasizing particularly its more intellectualist or
quasi-gnostic features. Thus he gives pride of place to such (gnostic-
sounding) verses of Scheffler as these:

To become nothing is to become God.
Nothingness swallows everything before it:
And if it does not swallow you,
You can never be born in eternal light.

Or again these lines:

I am like God, and God like me.
I am as great as God; He as small as I;
He cannot be above me, I not under Him.

Derrida expressly accentuates this outlook—called here an "apophatic" mysticism—while distancing it as far as possible from Christian *philia* or charity or love.[29] As in the case of Eckhart, however, one needs to guard here against a gnostic one-sidedness. As it happens, Scheffler himself distinguished between two kinds of spirituality, an intellectual and an erotic-mystical type, and he associated these two kinds with two angelic choirs: the "Cherubim," representing knowledge or intellect, and the "Seraphim," representing love. Although one of his main collections of poems is called "Cherubinic Wanderer" (*Cherubinischer Wandersmann*), he basically wanted to keep the two paths tied together. As he wrote: "Blessed are you if you are able to make room for both and if, in your earthly life, you sometimes burn with heavenly love like Seraphim, and sometimes focus your mental eye steadily on God like Cherubim." As a wanderer or pilgrim, Scheffler basically followed in the footsteps of St. Bonaventure's *itinerarium mentis in Deum*; this path, for him, involved a purifying movement, an itinerary from humanity to divinity ("*durch die Menschheit zu der Gottheit*")—one followed in such a manner that one never forgets human finitude and the mediating role of Jesus.[30]

Islamic Spiritualities

When turning from Christian to Islamic spirituality, one notices many familiar themes but also a kind of sea change. A prominent similarity resides in the rich profusion of different spiritualities—varieties that are only loosely bundled together under the umbrella of "Sufism." Another similarity derives from the "Abrahamic legacy" shared by the two religions, a congruence manifest in the invocation of similar biblical stories and religious symbolisms. The sea change, on the other hand, has to do with the relatively greater prominence of gnostic or quasi-gnostic tendencies in the Islamic context. Several things may account for this divergence. One may be the relatively late arrival of Islam in the Middle East, at a time when gnosticism had already taken firm roots and acquired a broad religious following. Another important one has to do with the centrality of divine oneness (*tawhid*) and the absence of mediating features in Islam—a centrality that may encourage gnostic aspirations toward ultimate unification or fusion. Closely connected with this aspect is the different status of Jesus and Prophet Muhammad in the two religious traditions. On this score, it is perhaps more difficult to link the messenger of Islam with *agape* spirituality—although resources for such a linkage are surely not lacking.[31]

As indicated, Islam has historically displayed a variety of spiritual orientations; however, as in the Christian case, two stand out: a knowledge-based and a more love-based variety. Notwithstanding numerous variations, gnostic spirituality aims at the unification or identification of the human knower with divine Being or else with the empty "abyss" of the divine—an identification that, by its nature, is reserved for a select group endowed with the spark of *gnosis*. Given the restrictedness of this spark and its separation from the ordinary world of ignorance (*jahiliyya*), gnostic spirituality favors esotericism and a relatively secret transmission of doctrines, in accord with its emphasis on privileged insight or knowledge (*ma'rifa*). In contrast with this restrictive type, ordinary Muslim spirituality comprises and relies on a number of ingredients. In mainstream Sufism, knowledge or illumination is by no means ignored, but it is amplified and counterbalanced by reverence for God (*makhafa*) and compassionate love (*mahabbah*). Generally speaking, one might say that the latter two ingredients take the place of the focus on Jesus and his suffering in Christian *agape* mysticism. Fear of or reverence for God, in particular, guards against intellectual conceit and a self-righteous "self-deification" or identification with the divine. Pride of place in ordinary Sufism, however, goes to love (*mahabbah*), a love whose target—God or fellow human beings—remains ambivalent and undecided because sensible and supersensible, visible and invisible realms are here seen as analogous and lovingly reconciled in their difference.

In the Islamic context (as in the Christian), intellectual spirituality is not a compact movement, nor does it subscribe to a unified doctrine. Moreover, its social stance varies, adopting sometimes a more reclusive or purely contemplative, sometimes a more activist or intrusive (occasionally even a millennarian) cast. An exemplar of the former kind is the "Great Sheikh": Abu Bakr Muhammad Muhyi-d-Din, known as Ibn Arabi (1165–1240). The point here is not to claim that Ibn Arabi was a gnostic in any formal sense of the term or that his spirituality was exclusively of an intellectual or illuminationist type. The opposite is true. As in the case of some Christian mystics, one can say that Ibn Arabi's outlook was multifaceted and comprised a variety of strands, including the strand of love mysticism. As he actually stated at one point, for him love (*mahabbah*) and not knowledge (*ma'rifah*) was the summit of mysticism because it is love and not knowledge that truly reflects divine union (*tawhid*). And in his *Tarjuman al-Ashwaq* we read:

Mine is the religion of love.
Wherever His [God's] caravans turn,
The religion of love
Shall be my religion and my faith.[32]

Yet it is commonly agreed that, among Muslim mystics, Ibn Arabi is the most intellectual or that his thought places a strong, perhaps preeminent, emphasis on intellectualism. This emphasis is evident in his key concept of "*wahdat al-wujud*" (unity of Being), according to which there is only one divine reality in comparison with which all other finite beings are ultimately "nothing" or nonexistent. The task of the Sufi mystic honoring this doctrine is to recognize nonexistence as a finite being and to accept fusion with the divine.[33]

For our present purposes, it must suffice to consider briefly one text in which the intellectual element clearly prevails. The text is "Whoso knoweth Himself . . . ," taken from Ibn Arabi's *Treatise on Being* (*Risale-t-ul-wujudiyyah*). The point of the title is that "whosoever knows himself" properly knows himself as integral to, and coterminous with, divine reality or Being. Commenting on the Prophet's saying "I know my Lord by my Lord," Ibn Arabi states:

> The Prophet points out by that saying that thou art not thou: thou art He, without thou; not He entering into thee, nor thou entering into Him, nor He proceeding forth from thee, nor thou proceeding forth from Him. And it is not meant by this that thou art anything that exists or thine attributes anything that exist; but it is meant by it that thou never wast nor wilt be, whether by thyself or through Him or in Him or along with Him. Thou art neither ceasing to be nor still existing. *Thou art He*, without any of these limitations. Then if you know thine existence thus, then thou knowest God; and if not, then not.

In its zeal to celebrate the absolute unity (*tawhid*) of divine being, Ibn Arabi's text goes even beyond traditional gnostic formulas stressing the need for a self-emptying or a cessation of self in God. "Most of those 'who know God' (*al 'urraf*)," he writes,

> make ceasing of existence and the ceasing of that ceasing a condition of attaining the knowledge of God; but that is an error and a clear oversight. For the knowledge of God does not presuppose the ceasing of existence nor the ceasing of that ceasing. For things have *no* existence, and what does not exist cannot cease to exist. . . . Then if thou knoweth thyself without existence or ceasing to be, then thou knoweth God; and if not, then not.[34]

Aware of the boldness of these formulations, Ibn Arabi proceeds to answer some questions raised by skeptically inclined readers. One such question concerns precisely the idea of an absolute unity devoid of duality, two-ness or difference. "How," the questioner asks, "lies the way to union, when thou affirmest that there is no other beside Him, and a thing cannot be united to itself?" Ibn Arabi answers:

No doubt, there is in reality no union nor disunion, neither far nor near. For union is not possible except between two, and if there be but one, there can be no union nor division. For union requires two either similar or dissimilar. Then, if they are similar, they are equals, and if they are dissimilar, they are opposites; but He (whose name be exalted) spurns to have either an equal or an opposite. . . . So there is union without union, and nearness without nearness, and farness without farness.

Elaborating further on this thought, he explains:

Understand, therefore, that the knower's knowledge of himself is God's knowledge of Himself, because his soul is nothing but He. . . . And whoever attains to this state, his existence is no more, outwardly or inwardly, any but the existence of Him (whose name be exalted). . . . So if one say "I am God," then hearken to him, for it is God (whose name be exalted) saying "I am God," not he. . . . [Here] our discourse is only with him who has sight and is not born blind; for he who does not know himself is blind and cannot see. And until the blindness depart, he will not attain to these spiritual matters.[35]

What one may notice in this statement is the surreptitious reemergence of a duality or difference: the duality between knowledge and ignorance, between the knowledgeable few and the unknowing multitude.

Ibn Arabi's teachings have left a strong imprint on Islamic spirituality over the centuries. For the most part, his legacy has been contemplative and reclusive, giving rise mainly to esoteric Sufi orders hermetically sheltered from, and disdainful of, the mundane world. However, gnostic spirituality can also take a different turn: especially under the impact of a more traditional gnostic dualism, the distinction between the "knowers" and the ignorant, between the "godlike" and the ungodly, can foster violent aggression and quasi-millennarian militancy. An example is an early version of Ismailism, a gnostic-dualistic branch that flourished during the late Abbasid reign. In line with older Manichean teachings, this sect—according to some historians—sharply distinguished between the hidden, unknowable God or divine "abyss," on the one hand, and the material-bodily world seen as the work of an inferior demiurge, on the other. The task of gnostic believers was to achieve deification through affirming their superior knowledge while attacking and, if possible, eradicating the inferior world. The latter aim was particularly the goal of the esoteric order of the so-called Assassins, a secretive group of militants (also known as *batiniyyah* or "people of the inner truth" or *fida'iyyah* or "self-sacrificers"). According to historical reports—which are not uncontested—the Assassins wreaked havoc throughout the Muslim world, killing two Abbasid caliphs, several sultans, and hundreds, perhaps thousands, of others. Whatever the historical accuracy, the great al-Ghazali (1058–1111)—though himself a Sufi mystic but of a very different persuasion—felt moved to denounce the teachings of this sect and their leaders.[36]

Without denying the role of intellectual insight, major strands in Islamic spirituality have always accorded a central role to *makhafa* and *mahabbah*. For our present purposes, it must suffice to look briefly at the mystical poetry of Jalal ad-Din Rumi, the great and justly revered "mevlana" or "maulana" (1207–73, a bare generation after Ibn Arabi). Rumi's work, especially his *Mathnawi*, is a rich and multidimensional tapestry of ideas, symbols, and metaphors. Some of these ideas are surely gnostic or intellectual (perhaps Neoplatonic) in character. Thus one recalls his famous statement: "Every form you see has its archetype in the divine world, beyond space. If the form perishes, what does it matter, since its heavenly model is indestructible?" Occasionally one also finds in Rumi traces of the doctrine of the unity of ultimate reality ("*wahdat al-wujud*"). Thus we read:

> I am filled with you—
> Skin, blood, bone, brain, and soul.
> There's no room for lack of trust, or trust.
> Nothing in this existence but that existence.

Or consider these Zenlike phrases, echoing Meister Eckhart:

Praise to the emptiness that blanks out existence. Existence:
This place made from our love for that emptiness.
Yet somehow comes emptiness,
This existence goes.
Praise to that happening, over and over![37]

Yet, as in Eckhart's case, this is not the whole story. In Rumi's work, celebration of unity and ultimate disappearance in the divine is always counterbalanced, and perhaps outweighed, by *mahabbah*—a loving devotion that never forgets a remaining two-ness or difference, even in the very urgency of overcoming separation. For without a recognition of two-ness, and hence of human finitude, how could Rumi have written: "Love must have a little pain"? Or these lines: "O love, everyone gives thee names and titles—last night I named thee once more: 'Pain without remedy.'" In this connection, we may also wish to remember these lines:

When I remember your love,
I weep, and when I hear people
Talking of you, something in my chest,
where nothing much happens now,
moves as in sleep.

And here is his celebration of unity in two-ness, a poem dedicated to his beloved friend, Shams of Tabriz:

All our lives we've looked
into each other's faces.
That was the case today too.
How do we keep our love-secret?
We speak from brow to brow
and hear with our eyes.[38]

As is clear from his poetry, Rumi's mysticism was all-consuming and all-embracive. Setting aside rigid boundaries, he confined his love neither to God nor to his friend Shams (who ultimately vanished), but allowed his love to grow and percolate and ultimately include all his fellow creatures in the world. As he stated at one point: "How can one profess love for God, if one does not love and actively show love to fellow-beings?" Love (*mahabbah*) here begins to shade over into service and compassion—an engaged commitment to the well-being of humanity at large. Here are some of Rumi's truly ecumenical lines, reflecting an ecumenism of loving service—though lines unlikely to be well received by clerical literalists in any religion:

> Tell me, Muslims, what should be done?
> I don't know how to identify myself. I am
> neither Christian nor Jew, neither Pagan nor Muslim.
> I don't hail from the East or from the West.
> I am neither from land nor sea. . . .
> This being human is a guest house:
> every morning a new arrival. . . .
> Be grateful for whoever comes,
> because each has been sent
> as a guide from beyond.[39]

Toward Global Spirituality?

By way of conclusion, I want to reflect briefly on competing spiritualities and their social relevance, especially in the context of the contemporary "spiritual marketplace." The main issue emerging from the preceding discussion is the respective assessment of gnosis and *agape*, of esoteric-intellectual spirituality and of love- or service-based spirituality. Loosely speaking—and neglecting possible overlaps—gnostic spirituality may be said to invite one to solitary contemplation and a solitary merger with the divine (a merger reserved for the privileged few); by contrast, *agape* spirituality has a more active and outgoing slant, a slant potentially rupturing or transgressing all boundaries based on status, race, and ethnic or religious background. The former type insists on division or hierarchy (hence the pronounced dualism of traditional gnosticism), while the second seeks to combine or balance integration and difference.

Both kinds of spirituality have merits and also demerits. Esoteric spirituality fosters a withdrawal from social bonds, from the busy-ness of worldly affairs; it encourages a retreat into the kind of *"Abgeschiedenheit"* so dear to Eckhart, Angelus Silesius, and many other mystics—a retreat that alone seems able to shield the human spirit against conformism, consumerism, and rampant commodification. Seen from this esoteric vantage point, *agape* spirituality stands accused of promoting a meddlesome, managerial attitude—a danger that indeed inhabits many contemporary forms of pragmatism and social "welfarism."[40] Still, the respective dangers are probably not symmetrical. Although valuable in many ways, retreat into solitude can also shade over into solipsism, which, in turn, can engender selfishness or haughty self-indulgence. Martin Luther's and Zinzendorf's invectives against the arrogant conceit of self-righteous "knowers" should probably not be forgotten in this context—and actually deserve increased attention in an age marked by "technocracy" and "expertocracy." In the prevailing global situation, gnostic retreat also signals—or can be perceived to signal—an exit from global moral and political responsibility. Quite apart from the problem of elitism, one also needs to take into account the more aggressive and violent type of gnosticism represented historically by the "Assassins" (and in our time by jihadists and terrorists).

In light of these and related dangers, intellectual spirituality (in my view) urgently needs to be counterbalanced by, and perhaps subordinated to, more sober and world-open perspectives—especially the demands of *agape* and *mahabbah* (properly channeled by *makhafa*). There is an old Christian tradition—with clear parallels in Islam—called "contemplation in action" or the "mysticism of everyday life." In Matthew Ashley's view, such contemplative action deserves renewed affirmation in our world today because of its ability to overcome social barriers between rich and poor and also because of its tendency to break down an "elistist division of labor" between clergy and laypeople.[41] It is this kind of action or "everyday mysticism" that is the central trait of the four spiritual guides celebrated in the present book. It also was the hallmark of Erasmus's life and work; following in the footsteps of the Brethren of the Common Life, his practical orientation, gentled by *agape*, led him to privilege pious conduct (or *orthopraxis*) over dogmas and rituals, ecumenical peacemaking over doctrinal apologetics. A similar kind of everyday piety was also the guiding wellspring in the lifework of the Mahatma Gandhi—a guidepost evident in his commitment to "*karma yoga*" or spiritual praxis.

To illustrate the potential of a global and properly ecumenical spirituality in our time, I want to cite briefly the example of a prominent recent spokesman of cosmopolis: Dag Hammarskjöld, the renowned secretary general of the United Nations (1953–61). Addressing an assembly of the World Council of Churches soon after assuming office, Hammarskjöld pinpointed the meaning of contemplative action by stating that we must approach global issues from "two angles": first, there is "a need for practical action, helping underdeveloped countries to achieve such economic progress as would give them their proper share in the wealth of the world"; secondly, there is an equal "need for inspiration, for the creation of a spirit among the leaders of peoples which helps them to use the forces which they have to master, for peace and not for war." Roughly at the same time, Hammarskjöld penned a statement of personal faith that admirably linked traditional *agape* spirituality with commitment to contemporary service. He wrote:

> The explanation of how man should live a life of active social service in full harmony with himself as a member of the community of spirit, I found in the writings of those great medieval mystics for whom "self-surrender" had been the way of self-realization, and who in "singleness of mind" and "inwardness" had found strength to say *yes* to every demand which the needs of their neighbors made them face, and to say *yes* also to every fate life had in store for them. Love . . . for them meant simply an overflowing of the strength with which they felt themselves filled when living in true self-oblivion. And this love found natural expression in an unhesitant fulfillment of duty and in an unreserved acceptance of life, whatever it brought them personally of toil, suffering or happiness.[42]

Chapter Six

Emptiness and Compassion

Some Christian-Buddhist Encounters

Not long ago, the theologian Paul Knitter published a book titled *Without Buddha I Could Not Be a Christian*.[1] In its bold formulation, the book demonstrated the attraction Buddhism has for at least some Christian thinkers. The attraction is not one-sided. In 1984, at an East-West Religious Encounter in Honolulu, Japanese Buddhist philosopher Masao Abe invoked St. Paul's Epistle to the Philippians where he says (2:5–8): "Have this mind in you, which was also in Christ Jesus who, existing in the form of God, counted being on an equality with God not a thing to be grasped, but emptied himself taking the form of a servant. . . . He humbled himself, becoming obedient even unto death, the death on the cross." In Abe's readings, the self-emptying (*kenosis*) of Jesus must be taken quite radically: "We should understand the doctrine of Christ's *kenosis* to mean that Christ as the Son of God is *essentially* and *fundamentally* self-emptying or self-negating," that is, he did not merely disguise himself as or pretend to be a servant. For Abe, the self-emptying of Jesus permeates the entire Christian theology, entailing necessarily the "*kenosis* of God." As he wrote, "Without the self-emptying of God 'the Father,' the self-emptying of the Son of God is inconceivable. . . . In the case of God, *kenosis* is implied in the original nature of God, that is, his love."[2]

Consulting recent Christian theology, Abe found limited resonances of the notion of *kenosis* in prominent texts—for example, in
Karl Rahner's presentation of the crucifixion of Jesus as "the death of
God" and in Jürgen Moltmann's portrayal of Golgotha as "an event
in God." Among earlier resonances Abe pointed to the "*Nichts* or
Ungrund" (Nothing or Unground), as discussed by Meister Eckhart and Jakob Böhme.[3] However, his main concern was the parallel between *kenosis* and the central Buddhist notion of "*sunyata*"
(emptiness). "The ultimate reality for Buddhism," he noted, "is neither Being nor God but *sunyata*," which is "entirely unobjectifiable,
unconceptualizable, and unattainable by reason or will." The important point is that emptiness is not another "something" alongside
other things: It is "not only not Being or God, but also not emptiness
as distinguished from somethingness or fullness." The crux here is
the self-emptying character of *sunyata*, the fact that it "not only empties everything but also empties itself." To this extent, it is an ongoing
happening, a "total dynamic movement" of transformation—moreover a movement that does not occur "outside us" but one in which
we are completely embroiled and that profoundly transforms us.
Seen from this angle, Buddhist *sunyata* for Abe has a liberating and
ultimately a "soteriological" significance.[4]

In the following I want to explore the parallel suggested by Abe
by examining three distinct cases of Christian-Buddhist encounter
during the past half century: first, the meeting of Paul Tillich's dialectical theology with Japanese Buddhist thought; second, the dialogue
of Thomas Merton's transindividualism with Zen Buddhism; and
finally, the encounter of Raimon Panikkar's Vedantic thought with
the Buddhist "silence of God." All three cases, in my view, illustrate
or exemplify Abe's vision of soteriological praxis.

Paul Tillich

In the case of Paul Tillich, the encounter with Buddhism—and more
generally with other non-Abrahamic religions—was a relatively late
experience, gathering momentum basically in the last decade of his
life. This fact may seem surprising in view of the strong emphasis his

theology placed on the "correlation" (nonseparation) of all phenomena and beliefs. To be sure, none of his early works were marked by any kind of narrow confessionalism or provincialism. Yet one cannot ignore the roots of his work in Western thought, especially in early (individualistic) existentialism and liberal Protestantism. Thus the move toward Asian perspectives, and especially toward Japanese Zen Buddhism, required strong catalysts or motivating impulses. For Tillich, these impulses were provided by meetings with the great Zen masters Daisetz Suzuki (1870–1966) and Shin'ichi Hisamatsu (1889–1980) in the 1950s. Suzuki at that time was teaching at Columbia University (when Tillich was at Union Theological Seminary), while Hisamatsu served as a visiting professor at Harvard (where Tillich moved in 1955). These meetings, especially the conversations with Hisamatsu, proved a kind of turning point for the theologian. As his secretary reported: "The visit of the great Japanese Zen Master, Hisamatsu, created more than a mild stir at Harvard. . . . His several visits with Professor Tillich bore out my feeling that this encounter was deeply stirring to the theologian."[5]

Many of the conversations between Tillich and Hisamatsu have been recorded, transcribed, and finally published, bringing to the fore many important convergences and divergences. What both men shared was an attitude of open-mindedness and willingness to learn, an openness felt to be imperative in the context of global secularization. What divided or at least distinguished them were their respective views of the status of individuality or particular existence in relation to the broader religious framework. Whereas for Tillich the particular individual had an ontological status and even served as a "pivotal theme" in Christianity, Hisamatsu did not find this status compelling. The Zen master here turned to the centrality of self-emptying (*sunyata*) in Buddhist thought, stating that—in view of the nonsubstantiality of the self—there is actually "neither self nor other," "neither self nor world," leaving behind only a "selfless" self and a "formless" universe. For Tillich this conclusion was challenging and even ethically provocative. In the words of Tillich scholar Marc Boss, the theologian needed to hold firm "the ethical valuation of the individual over against his devaluation" and also "the personal character of divinity over against the idea of a transpersonal absolute."

In the course of further conversations, Hisamatsu tried to persuade Tillich that nonsubstantiality or nonduality was not reducible to an undifferentiated sameness or identity—with only limited success. As the theologian finally admitted: "I must try to learn with my dualistic mind how the individual or 'particular' is simultaneously preserved and not preserved" in Buddhist *sunyata*.[6]

The issue at that point was not resolved. Coming from a Christian theological as well as a Western philosophical background, Tillich had difficulty extricating himself from the opposition between sameness (identity) and difference (as separation). What ego transgression meant from this angle was at most a "participation" in a shared concern. But was this Buddhist nonduality? During 1960, Tillich spent some ten weeks in Japan, traveling to several places but meeting especially with Suzuki in Kamakura and with Hisamatsu in Kyoto. His conversations with the Zen masters are recorded in an "Informal Report" written by the theologian. What emerges from the report is again the crucial significance Tillich attributed to the distinction between sameness (identity) and mutual participation, between wholeness and particularity. Presenting this distinction as the fundamental contrast between Christianity and Buddhism, and more broadly between West and East, Tillich states in the report: "The discussions with the Buddhists have shown me that their main points of difference with Christianity are always the different valuation placed on the individual, the meaning of history, interpersonal relations. . . . It is the contrast between the principle of identity and the principle of participation." Also of considerable importance to Tillich in his Japanese encounters was the role of devotional piety, especially of prayer, in Buddhism. As he stated in another context: "I can understand how it is that a Jew, a Christian or a Muslim prays, because praying always leads people to another ego, a Thou, and it is thus an ego-thou relationship. . . . But on the other hand, in the official doctrine and theological background of Buddhism, the personal element is almost swallowed up by the suprapersonal element"—which leads to the basic question: "To whom does a Buddhist pray if he prays instead of meditating?"[7]

Following his visit to Japan, in the fall of 1961 Tillich presented a series of lectures (called Bampton Lectures) at Columbia University under the title "Christianity and the Encounter of the World Religions." As one will note, the emphasis of the title was placed on "Christian" encounter (not the other way around). As Tillich stated in the opening pages of the printed lectures, his aim was "to discuss the topic from the point of view of Christianity"—although his stance was not that of an "outsider" but of a "participant observer" who investigates common "elements in human nature" that may give rise to different symbols in different religions. The third lecture in the series was titled "A Christian-Buddhist Conversation," with a focus deriving from the character of Buddhism as "one of the greatest, strangest, and most competitive of the religions proper." As in the case of other encounters, for Tillich the dialogical relation between the two religions relied on a number of presuppositions: the mutual recognition of the value of the respective perspectives, the firm rootedness of the dialogue partners in their respective traditions, and the sincere search for a common ground that "makes both dialogue and conflict possible." Another crucial predisposition was the orientation of the dialogue partners to the ultimate goal or *telos* of religious faith and the "intrinsic aim of existence." In Tillich's words: "It is *here* that one should start every inter-religious discussion, and not with a comparison of contrasting [abstract] concepts of God or man."[8]

Having laid down the basic parameters of the encounter, Tillich immediately zeroes in on the basic difference between the two religions, a difference having to do with their respective conceptions of their *telos* or goal. As he writes: "In Christianity, the *telos* of everyone and everything is united in [the vision of] the Kingdom of God; in Buddhism the *telos* of everything and everyone is fulfilled in Nirvana." From this distinction derive a whole host of theoretical and practical differences. While the Christian Kingdom of God is "a social, political, and personalistic symbol" oriented toward a "reign of justice and peace," the Buddhist Nirvana is "an ontological symbol" that, reacting to the human experience of finitude, separation, and suffering, postulates "the blessed oneness of everything, beyond finitude and error." Both religions stand opposed to an existential negativity or default: while the Christian *telos* opposes itself to the kingdoms of *this* world, that is, the "demonic power structures" ruling history and personal life, the Buddhist Nirvana denounces the grip of appearances and illusions as contrasted to *sunyata*, seen as the "ground of Being" or genuine reality. But even here differences surface. Whereas in Christianity the negative judgment is directed against the world "in its existence, not its essence"—that is, against the fallen, not the "created" world—Buddhist negation targets the apparent world, which is "the result of an ontological fall into finitude."[9]

For Tillich, the most important differences between the two religions arise, however, in the domains of ethics and history. To highlight these differences, he invokes again the two conceptions of "participation" and "identity." In the case of the Christian *telos*, he argues, the assumption is that one participates "as an individual being" in the coming Kingdom of God; on the other hand, by canceling all particularities, the Buddhist Nirvana entails that everybody is "identical" with everybody and everything else. By accepting the separation of particularity from ultimate oneness, Christianity sometimes lends support to Western aspirations of technical mastery in which nature becomes "a tool for human purposes"—a danger avoided by the Buddhist embrace of "identity." This aspect, however, is more than compensated for, in Tillich's view, by ethical and historical considerations. In a "considerably condensed" formulation, he states, participation leads to "*agape*," whereas identity merely fuels "compassion." In the biblical sense, *agape* is the attitude that "accepts the unacceptable and tries to transform it," thereby changing everything in the direction of God's Kingdom. By contrast, compassion (*karuna*) for Tillich neither accepts nor transforms the other but only cosuffers through identification. What is lacking is the will to change others either directly or indirectly "by transforming the sociological and psychological structures by which they are conditioned." This leads to a basic historical divergence. The Christian *telos* is future-oriented, envisaging "a new heaven and a new earth"; this means that the symbol of the Kingdom of God has "a revolutionary character." By contrast, in Buddhism "not transformation of reality but salvation from reality is the basic attitude." Differently phrased: under the aegis of Buddhist compassion, "no transformation of society as a whole, no aspiration for the radically new in history," can be contemplated.[10]

These considerations lead Tillich finally to a crucial social-political implication: namely, regarding the feasibility of democracy.

As he reminds readers, Western democracy was imposed on Japan following the latter's defeat in World War II. Although it was "accepted" by the Japanese, the question is this: what was the basis of this acceptance (except military defeat)? Tillich believes that Western democracy has a clear foundation anchored in Christian faith: namely, the recognition of every individual as a distinct person, as "a being of infinite value and equal rights in view of the Ultimate." Such a recognition is not found anywhere in Japanese tradition (in either Buddhism or Shintoism). Thus, although Japan may "accept" and even "want" democracy, it is stymied by the lack of spiritual grounding; its leaders know "that Buddhism is unable to furnish such a foundation." At this point, to Tillich's own chagrin, the conversation launched in the cited lecture stalled or came to "a preliminary end." However, one may ask: is this stalling inevitable? Clearly much depends here on the meaning of "democracy." Tillich's version—which he strenuously upheld throughout his life—seems to concur roughly with a certain conception of "liberal democracy," a conception foregrounding the distinctness, separation, and "autonomy" of the individual participants. By construing the Buddhist Nirvana as nondifferentiation, sameness, or "identity," this version clearly places Buddhism beyond the democratic pale. But again: is this contrast exhaustive? Is there not an alternative to both the "dualism" of separation and the "monism" of identity? Differently put: might there not be a "kenotic" democracy?[11]

Thomas Merton

To explore the latter possibility—or at least take some steps in this direction—it may be appropriate to turn attention at this point to another Christian thinker roughly of the same generation: the Cistercian monk Thomas Merton. Like Tillich, Merton was a prolific author, producing a large number of scholarly, literary, and poetic writings. Again like Tillich, in his later life he ventured beyond the bounds of Western and Abrahamic religions in the direction of Asian, especially Buddhist, spirituality. For our present purposes, I confine myself to his book *Mystics and Zen Masters*, written and first published in 1967 at the Abbey of Gethsemani. In his foray into Buddhist thought, Merton (again like Tillich) was aided by the teachings of leading Zen masters, especially Daisetz Suzuki and Shin'ichi Hisamatsu, and also other Buddhists like Masao Abe and Thich Nhat Hanh. As he writes in his preface, the aim of his book was not to produce a Buddhist dogmatics or an "abstract metaphysics"; rather, its pages are animated by one central concern: "to understand how people of different traditions have conceived the meaning and method of the 'way' (*tao*) which leads to the highest levels of religious or metaphysical awareness." The path here is difficult, for "there is more to human life than just 'getting somewhere' or getting ahead." In fact, "the highest ambition lies beyond ambition, in the renunciation of the 'self' that seeks its own aggrandizement." To move along this path requires "a certain 'purification' of the will and intelligence."[12]

In a central chapter of his book, Merton explores the status of selfhood and individual freedom, especially as this status was shaped by the current of "existentialism" prevalent in the West in the middle of the twentieth century. Basically, the aim of his exploration is twofold. On the one hand, he defends individuality and personal freedom against the onslaught of modern "mass society," in which everything is submerged in an anonymous collectivity (what Heidegger had called "*das Man*"). On the other hand, he makes an effort to rescue existentialist thought from the danger of a self-centered (and anthropocentric) solipsism by guiding it toward the acceptance of genuine social and communal bonds. For Merton the chief problem of modernity is the peril of "massification" and dehumanization; here the rebellious side of existentialism rightly comes to the fore. In his words: "Traditional metaphysics, whether realist or idealist, is interested in the question *what* (the essence). Existentialism wants to know *who*; it is interested in the authentic use of freedom by the concrete person." This freedom, to be sure, cannot in turn be objectified but has to show forth in action. Thus the existentialist *telos* is "found in personal self-realization, that is, in practical freedom, in responsibility and authentic personhood." Taking a leaf from Albert Camus, and partly from Sartre, in the chapter Merton states that the existentialist is "condemned" to be free: "He is a rebel, an individualist who, because he withdraws from the common endeavor of technological society," may end up in futility and despair. The conclusion drawn from this withdrawal by the modern mass media is that nonconformity is in a way fatal: not to submit to the "leveling" of mass society is tantamount to an exit from social life.[13]

In rebelling against mass conformism, however, Merton's idea of freedom does not necessarily end up in isolation and despair. Human freedom does indeed involve selfhood but also the transcendence of self or self-transgression. Existential decision, Merton writes, does indeed proceed from "autonomy" (vis-à-vis mass society) but also involves acceptance of "finiteness, one's own limitations, in fact, one's own 'nothingness'"—though a nothingness that is not purely negative or destructive but rather liberating because it makes room for nonegocentric involvement, a presence in "the actions of the real world." Seen from this angle, existentialism is not self-centered, not "a withdrawal into privacy or unworldliness"; it is not "monastic" but rather socially involved and "open" to the needs of others. Basically, what existentialist thought has tried to accomplish is to replace "a fraudulent world of inauthentic and illusory relationships" with a genuine interhuman bond. For Merton this brings into view two contrasting conceptions of community: on the one hand, there is "a false and arbitrary fiction, a collective togetherness in which all possibility of authentic existence is surrendered"; on the other hand, we find "a genuine community of persons who have accepted their fragile lot and . . . the solitude of the person who must think and decide for himself/herself." Only between such free persons is "true communication" possible. Differently phrased: "The authentic person is not born in Stoic isolation but in the openness and dialogue of love." The final question that arises here is the "grounding" of a selfless selfhood, of a nothingness that does not destroy but liberates and sustains. Taking some cues from religiously inspired existentialists (like Karl Jaspers and Gabriel Marcel), Merton turns to the notion of a "groundless grounding" that is not humanly fabricated but is received as a divine dispensation. Here Sartre's blank nothingness (*le néant*) emerges as the "abyss of a divine gift": "The self is 'void' indeed, but void in the sense of the apophatic mystics like St. John of the Cross in whom the *nada* or nothingness of the self—empty of fictitious projects and desires—becomes *todo*, the All."[14]

Pursuing a similar line of thought, Merton in other parts of his book turns to mystical religious teachings, especially to the teachings of Zen Buddhism. In a chapter titled "Mystics and Zen Masters" he takes to task a conception that views Buddhism as anchored in individual inwardness and a retreat into "unworldliness." He asks, "Is Zen meditation aimed at a purification of the self by rejection of the material world and of 'external' concerns in order to seek fulfillment in pure interiority?" Responding to this query, he finds "absolutely no evidence" for such a construal. In fact, what he intends to question is the very idea "that Zen meditation is simply a rest in individual 'essence' which abolishes all need for and interest in external and historical reality, or the destiny of man." In even stronger terms, he denounces as "quite false" the image of Zen as "a sort of individualistic, subjective enterprise," as "a subtle form of spiritual self-gratification, a repose in the depths of one's own inner silence." For Merton, the "first and most elementary fact about Zen" is its abhorrence of any dualism, especially the dualisms of spirit and matter, subject and object. What this rejection entails is a search for a realm beyond all binary oppositions, even beyond the dualism of the "I-Thou" relationship (which still presupposes subjects). Tersely put: Zen seeks "enlightenment" that results from the resolution of all binary relations and oppositions in a "pure void" or emptiness (*sunyata*)—a void that is not a static negativity but dynamically empties itself of the void. "One might say," Merton writes, "that Zen is the ontological awareness of pure Being beyond subject and object, an immediate grasp of Being in its 'suchness' or 'thusness.'" This awareness is "not reflective, not self-conscious, not philosophical, not theological"; for want of a better term, one might call it "purely spiritual."[15]

To illustrate and further profile the depth of Zen, Merton turns to (what he calls) "the most critical moment in the history of Chinese Zen": the encounter between the Sixth Patriarch, Hui Neng (founder of the "southern school"), and his competitor Shen Hsui (founder of the "northern school") in the seventh century. The encounter, or rather dispute, revolved around the "mirror-wiping Zen," that is, the conception that enlightenment is reached by an effort to wipe the mind clean. Shen Hsui believed that the approach to Nirvana required an act of introversion, a turning to internal consciousness assisted by formal meditation (especially "just sitting," *zazen*) and resulting in a pure mind purged of illusions. In Merton's words, for Shen Hsui Zen enlightenment or "seeing" consisted in "awareness of a primal mirror-like purity" in which the mind's inner "light" is the basis upon which enlightenment rests. By contrast, the Sixth Patriarch thought that nothing was further from Zen than the "mysticism of introversion." As Merton states (to some extent following Suzuki), Hui Neng "revolutionized" Buddhism by discounting formalized practices of "mirror-wiping." By the same token, far from being a "quietist," Hui Neng reacted *"against* any quietistic type of spirituality"—without becoming simply "activistic." According to Merton, the patriarch rejected two main assumptions: first, the assumption of the primacy of "a central ego-consciousness, an 'I' which, with all good intentions, sets out to 'achieve liberation or enlightenment,'" and second, the assumption that the inner self or the mirroring mind is a "possession," something "we own." What happens here, Merton comments, is that "possessive ego-consciousness" craftily outwits or circumvents *sunyata*. Basically, emptiness itself is treated as a possession or "attainment"; the "spiritualized ego enjoys its own narcissism under the guise of emptiness."[16]

Merton here refers to the famous statement of the First Patriarch, Bodhidharma: "All the attainments of the Buddhism are really non-attainments." Accordingly, the basis of enlightenment for Hui Neng is neither the ego nor the "mirror-wiping" mind but rather the "grounding unground," the ultimate reality that (as Merton says) is "at once pure Being and pure awareness." Contrasting it to the conscious ego, Hui Neng calls it the "ultimate mind" or the "unconscious" (*wu nien*)—which is equivalent to the Sanskrit *prajña* or wisdom. From the angle of this *prajña*-wisdom, emptiness achieved through mirror-wiping is "nothing but a trick" or "bogus mysticism." True emptiness or liberation occurs only when the *prajña*-unground shows itself forth, when it "breaks through our ego consciousness and floods with its intelligibility not only our whole being but all things that we see and know around us." At this point, "we are transformed in the *prajña*-light, we 'become' that light which in fact we are."[17] At this juncture, Merton finds it possible to build a bridge between Zen

Buddhism and certain forms of Christian mysticism. "In my opinion," he writes, "the contemplation of the void (*sunyata*) as described by Hui Neng has definite affinities with well-known records of Christian mystical experience." Thus the statement in John's gospel about "the light which enlightens every man coming into this world" (John 1:9) corresponds "pretty closely" to the notion of *prajña* and Hui Neng's "unconscious." Likewise, the "Spiritual Way" recommended by St. John of the Cross is "falsely conceived" as a plea for introversion; rather, it entails that "the light of God shines in all emptiness where there is no natural subject to receive it." Thus "to enter the Way is to leave the Way."[18]

As one can see, liberation in Hui Neng's Zen has a double character, liberating the practitioner from both external and internal compulsions, from the constraints of mass society as well as from the impulses of the ego. Thus, to rephrase the point, Buddhist liberation transgresses the subject-object dichotomy by opening the realm of *prajña*. In Merton's words: "The illumination of the Hui Neng school is a breakthrough which does not simply produce an enlightened state of consciousness or super-consciousness in the experience of the individual, but which allows Being itself to reveal its light, which is no light and void." To capture this breakthrough, customary terminology tends to fail: it is neither activistic nor quietistic; it is a passive activity, a doing by not doing (*wu wei*). To this extent, it seems similar to what Tillich called "theonomy" (and closely akin to what Heidegger called "letting-be"). To listen again to Merton: "It is a liberation from *all* forms of bondage to techniques, to exercises, to systems of thought and spirituality, to specific forms of individual spiritual achievement, to limited and dogmatic programs." The "unground" of Being is both Light (enlightenment) and pure Act. In the process of disclosure, Light and self-emptying Act are, so to speak, "let loose in pure freedom and power to give and maintain in action this self which is no-self, this void (*sunyata*) that is the inexhaustible source of all light and act." Once this disclosure has broken into our own lives, bursting its limitations, "we are lost in the boundless freedom and energy of *prajña*-wisdom."[19]

By venturing into the domain of *prajña*-wisdom, Merton leaves behind Tillich's reservations regarding the supposed nonindividualism or anti-individualism of Buddhism. He also leaves behind Tillich's portrayal of Nirvana as a faceless void and of *sunyata* as an undifferentiated "identity"—given that the "unground" is not "identifiable." Most important, Merton does not share Tillich's quandary regarding the compatibility or (rather) incompatibility of Buddhism and democracy. Clearly, the latter is not obviated but instead profoundly strengthened by the "boundless freedom and energy" of *prajña*-wisdom. This point is underscored in the concluding chapter of Merton's book, titled "Buddhism and the Modern World." Relying on Suzuki and Hisamatsu, Merton there asserts that the deepest aspiration of Zen, and of Buddhism in general, is emancipation: more specifically, the "ultimate emancipation from duality," which entails a "self-sustaining independence." Accordingly, the "attainment of Buddhahood" is not the imitation of a Buddha (existing somewhere else) but the awakening to the ground of Being or to "the Buddha which one is." In the vocabulary of Zen, "true self" designates not a self-centered ego or a possessive individual but rather the "formless original mind, the void or *sunyata*." Elaborating on this point, Merton invokes again Suzuki, who "explicitly compared this concept to that of the Godhood of Meister Eckhart and the Rhenish mystics." In a bold interpretation, the text also finds a parallel between the concept and the Marxist notion of alienation and its overcoming, stating that only a grasp of no-self reveals "the real implications of Marx's teaching on alienation and on the ultimate freedom which communism is supposed to bring about." The grasp is far removed from the "pseudo-freedom" of those who have "bypassed illumination" and arrived at "pure autonomy" in unregenerate selfishness.[20]

What frequently obstructs understanding here is the equation of *sunyata* with a pure negativity that itself is objectified and thus rendered oppressive. Rejecting this misconstrual, Merton insists that Zen "does not resolve all being into a pure void, but sees the void itself as an inexhaustible source of creative dynamism" or dynamic creativity. Far from reducing everything to nullity or sameness, Zen appreciates coherent diversity, facilitating "apprehension of the One in the Many, of the void in everyday life"—thus laying the foundation for a "Zen humanism" in our world today. Following Hisamatsu, in this final chapter Merton recognizes two derailments or pitfalls in contemporary thinking: that of "a degenerate, irrational, purely will-ful and anthropocentric humanism" and that of "a return to ancient traditional and mythical concepts which leaves no room for human autonomy at all." While the former bears characteristic traits of West-ern "liberalism," the latter is sometimes a temptation for Buddhism (and other religions as well). In Merton's words: "Traditional Bud-dhism, formal, rigid, doctrinaire, is sterile, fit for the museum, irrele-vant in the modern world, not because it is out of touch with current realities, but because it is *out of touch with human experience itself.*"[21]

To illustrate the dynamic, progressive, and democratic poten-tial of Buddhism, Merton in the end refers to the Vietnamese monk Thich Nhat Hanh, head of a militant movement for peace and jus-tice in the world. For the Vietnamese, he points out, Buddhism is not a doctrine; rather, it arises out of the basic human experience of suffering (*dukkha*), and its point is to provide "a realistic answer to the most urgent human question: how to cope with suffering?" Such coping is rendered impossible as long as people resort to such illusory devices as "party, race, nation, and even official religion" as protective shields. These illusory devices must be shattered for people to come to grips with their basic ailment. From Nhat Hanh's angle: "Pierc-ing the illusions which divide us, Buddhism must enable us to attain unity or solidarity with our brothers/sisters through openness and compassion, endowed with secret resources of creativity." This love or compassion can "transform the world" by operating not from out-side but in and through us.[22]

Raimon Panikkar

The need to overcome suffering and divisions, so strongly empha-sized by Nhat Hanh, was also a main concern of the philosopher of religion (and Catholic priest) Raimon Panikkar. As in the case of Tillich and Merton, Panikkar took an approach to faith and religious teachings that was not primarily cognitive or abstractly theological but experiential: the outgrowth of existential agony and striving. As is evident from the long string of his publications, his effort was always to explore the relevance, or else the irrelevance, of religious belief in the context of the contemporary age, an age marked largely by secularism, agnosticism, and anthropocentrism. Curiously, again like Tillich and Merton, in the 1960s Panikkar turned to Asian Buddhism, a tradition that strangely seems to hover on the cusp of theism and atheism, of faith and no-faith. Perhaps even more strongly than in the other two cases, his turn was propelled by personal experience: the son of an Indian father and a Spanish mother, his outlook was shaped by both Christian faith and classical Hindu teachings, with the latter not too far removed from Buddhist insights. To accentuate even more the existential basis of his turn: the 1960s saw the height of the Cold War, a conflict pitting against each other a largely theistic West and a nontheistic or atheistic (in this case, communist) East. At least in part, the agony of this conflict was behind one of Panikkar's major writings at the time: *The Silence of God: The Answer of the Buddha*.[23]

As Panikkar states at the beginning of his study, his main effort was to illuminate contemporary dilemmas and especially to build a bridge between the "religious preoccupation with atheism" (in the West) and the message of the Buddha, which, to all appearances, "leaves no room for God." The effort was complicated and nearly frustrated by the prevalent view of Buddhism (again in the West) as "an atheistic, nihilistic, negative religion" (yoked with some polytheistic features derived from Hinduism). Although it was gradually becoming recognized in some quarters that Buddhism is "neither theistic nor atheistic," still the notion of an "atheistic religion" was paradoxical and bewildering to most people. To make some headway in this domain, Panikkar first offers an overview of current popular assessments of "Buddha's faith" and especially of his "silence" on ultimate issues. One widespread opinion is expressed by the charge of cynicism, according to which the Buddha was a charlatan who either simulated faith or dissimulated it for ulterior motives. Closely related to this view is the charge of nihilism, according to which Buddha was in fact a thoroughgoing atheist who preached an absolute negativism. A bit more nuanced is the claim of agnosticism, according to which the Buddha professed ignorance about final issues out of a prudent acknowledgment of human finitude. Although acknowledging some hints of truth in these interpretations, Panikkar ultimately does not accept any of them. Rather, his own view moves in the direction of "apophaticism," the latter taken in a strong sense. As he writes: "The ultimate reason for the Buddha's silence is rooted neither in the inherent limitation of the human mind, nor in the imperfection of our cognition nor in the 'mysterious' nature of reality." Instead, the basic reason resides in the fact that this ultimate reality "*is not.*" The "is not" here has the meaning of *kenosis* or *sunyata*. This means that what is at issue, for Panikkar, is not merely a cognitive claim that ultimate reality is *ineffable*. Rather, Buddhist apophaticism transplants ineffability into the heart of ultimate reality itself, declaring that this reality "is ineffable not merely in our regard, but as such, *quoad se.*" Thus Buddhist apophaticism is an "*ontological* apophaticism."[24]

Based on this interpretation, Panikkar in the rest of his study proceeds with the task of bridge-building needed in our time. What this task involves is not merely a theoretical "comparison" between mutually indifferent perspectives but rather a serious engagement, a cross-fertilization and even "symbiosis" between religions East and West. The bridge or link, for Panikkar, is the seemingly paradoxical notion of an "atheistic religion" (or religious a-theism). The Buddha, he states, did not deny the ultimate reality of divine mystery but refused to substantialize it in a cognitive formula; rather, he addressed himself to "the ultimate end of religion: salvation [from suffering], showing others the way." A similar outlook may pervade a nascent "religious atheism" in the West. In articulating the emerging situation, Panikkar boldly goes beyond Tillich (and perhaps even Merton). Basically, he believes that the present age harbors a new "kairological" and even "axial" potential for human experience. As he writes: "I acknowledge in so-called contemporary 'atheism' a new, urgent phenomenon of the first magnitude, one of the great moments of humanity, deserving to be placed alongside the sixth century before the Christian era" (the axial age). What the term "atheism" here involves is not a simple denial of God (in the sense of popular "death of God" formulas) but rather the abandonment of a theism that treats God as omnipotent power and heteronomous master. "The new phenomenon," Panikkar states, "is that those who declare themselves believers define themselves as unbelievers [in this kind of deity] by living with scarcely any reference to a [heteronomous] transcendence." In the new situation, the old boundaries are either erased or redrawn: "This atheism 'saves' human beings from the clutches of transcendence as from the quick sands of immanence, delivering them from the opposition of superstition as from the [positivist] credulity of the sciences."[25]

Elaborating further on the kairological moment of the present, Panikkar sketches a new constellation of different but nonseparate elements: God, world, and humanity. "My hypothesis," he writes, "which I advance only as a humble hermeneutic, comes to this: the heart and essence of what until now has been called 'atheism' . . . is not a mere opposition to tenuous propositions regarding the existence of a Supreme Being." This would merely be reactive. Rather, it represents "a new stage along the journey of humanity, a new degree of awareness" comparable to that achieved in the axial age. What emerges is the insight—apophatically speaking—that there "is" no God, just as there "is" no humankind. This means "neither that the creature is nothing and God is all," nor "that the creature is all and God is nothing," nor "that there is a little cavity for the created in the bosom of divinity." The older terminology no longer suffices: "In others words, neither monism nor dualism—neither pantheism, nor atheism, nor theism—corresponds to the profound experience that people in our time seek to express." A new correlation or constellation is emerging: "The world, humankind, and God are, as it were, incompatible as three separate, independent entities. They are intertwined"—beyond sameness and separation. This is what Panikkar at other places has expressed in the quasi-trinitarian formula of "cosmotheandrism." The important point is that none of the elements is objectified, substantialized, or absolutized. As he adds: "The challenge of the present age will be to examine whether it is possible to 'de-divinize' Being and 'de-ontologize' God, without either one suffering any detriment."[26]

An important corollary of de-substantialization is the readiness of the emerging perspective to take "nothingness" or nonbeing seriously—in the sense not only of a logical negation but of the absence of being coupled with the absence or negation of nonbeing. In Panikkar's words: "God is the one who is absent, and always absent, to the point that were God ever indeed to appear, the divine essence would not be of the divine essence, but only a manifestation, a veil, the mere shadow and outline of God's being, a pre-essence." Sharpening the point, he adds: "God 'is' not only Being, but also Non-Being. . . . Strictly speaking God is beyond Being and Non-Being." This, of course, is at the heart of apophaticism, which involves a speaking in the language of silence. From this angle, no words can be adequate to their "object"; hence God is always "absent." In stirring language, some of it borrowed from scripture, Panikkar elaborates: "A God who is not absent will be a simple idol, *Resurrexit, non est hic*! (Matthew 28:6)." In a sense, God is a "*utopos*," being "no-where, in no place"; God's figurative presence is only "for making God's absence, God's *ab-esse*, noticed." Differently stated, "*ecstasy*, emergence from oneself, loss of being, genuine *ek-stasis*, is the only path to the attainment of the Absent One and the achievement of oneness with the Absent One." But again: Non-Being or absence also "nothings" itself (emptiness empties itself). Hence the apophatic turning: "It is precisely absence that permits presence. . . . Absence 'is' not; but it is what permits to-be; it makes it possible for presence to appear." Simply put: "God can be beyond Being only if the presence of Being is not that of a positivity but simply that of a lack. And here we are once more at the core of Buddhism" or the Buddha's silence.[27]

The emphasis on absence and apophasis does not lead Panikkar to neglect the other crucial aspect of Buddhism: the stress on suffering and relief from suffering through compassion (*karuna*). On the contrary, precisely when all elements are "de-substantialized" and freed from fixed being does liberating and nondomineering engagement become possible. Admittedly, this is a difficult thought. "It is objected," Panikkar observes, "if the spiritual end of humankind is the loss of self, should we not perhaps think that all other beings are likewise 'nothingness'? But if human beings and the world are nothingness, what need is there to concern ourselves with them?" However, this is a non sequitur. Precisely by being devoid of self-centeredness are human beings able to engage in caring praxis and to nurture selfless compassion. In fact, in Mahayana Buddhism (which includes Zen), showing "great compassion" (*mahakaruna*) is preferable to Nirvana itself, or at least a corollary of the latter. The Buddha's own praxis, anchored in his freedom, by no means seeks to advance his own status or influence; his *karuna* resides in "the superabundance of his state of 'grace.'" Far from being confined to himself, his "superabundant love overflows upon one's fellow beings, without any other intent than the well-being of these persons and the alleviation of the burden of their earthly pilgrimage." Free from authoritarianism and also paternalism, the Buddha seeks to "let" people "be" in the best possible way; he wishes to lead people little by little "to an elimination of the suffering in which we are plunged at every step along the pathway of life."[28]

At this point, Panikkar joins Thich Nhat Hanh (and also Merton) in accentuating liberating praxis over cognition (or *gnosis*), including liberating social praxis. What saves us, he writes, is the refusal to entertain any doctrine or ideology that pretends to deliver authoritative "knowledge" of God. Rather, "what is of true value, what carries us beyond the nearer shore of ours is *orthopraxis*," the willingness to follow the path (the "eightfold path") of right conduct (*dharma*). In following this path, we can rely on the example of the Buddha; but we can also have recourse to the larger community of followers (*sangha*) and their solidarity. In maintaining silence on ultimate matters, the Buddha wished not to confuse, bewilder, or distress his followers but rather to "liberate" them, both individually and in the larger social community. What is left behind on this liberating path are the compulsions both of a divine "heteronomy" and a self-centered human "autonomy." In a creative variation of Tillich's notion of "theonomy," Panikkar proposes the idea of "ontonomy" and of an "ontonomic" praxis seeking to deliver both "from the apotheosis of an exterior God and from the divinization of the human element." Ultimately, the preaching of the Buddha points to a "profound freedom" both individually and socially, a freedom that has no truck with caprice or libertinism. Thus the Buddha's teachings—and also his silence—are directed toward "complete liberation, a deliverance from both external coercion and interior will" (to power).[29] This, in turn, paves the way toward a released humanity no longer entrapped in aggressive individual or collective identities.[30]

Epilogue

On Being Poor in Spirit

Following the preceding chapters on spirituality and spiritual guides, it seems appropriate to conclude with a reminder: spirituality is not simply a human faculty, a kind of fullness or possession. Rather, it denotes a basic lack or emptiness, a dispossession that prompts an intense yearning or solicitation. Only a person who has deeply experienced this emptiness can seriously pray: "Come Holy Spirit, fill the hearts of your faithful and kindle in them the fire of your love." No one has described this experience more eloquently than the Rhenish mystic Meister Eckhart.

The gospel of Matthew (5:3–10) offers a list of "beatitudes" or benedictions pronounced by Jesus during his sojourn in Galilee. The first benediction is this: "Blessed are the poor in spirit, for theirs is the kingdom of heaven." That benediction is followed by blessings on "those who mourn," on "the meek," on "those who hunger and thirst for righteousness," on "the pure in heart," on "the peacemakers," and on those "persecuted for righteousness's sake." But the first blessing goes to the "poor in spirit." What does that mean? Interestingly, the gospel of Luke (6:20–23) also offers a list of benedictions, but the first is simply "Blessed are the poor" (*Beati pauperes*). This seems to be straightforward. But what about the statement in Matthew?

Among the sermons delivered by Meister Eckhart is one (Sermon 32) titled *"Beati pauperes spiritu"* ("Blessed Are the Poor in Spirit").[1] Could we also say here "poor in spirituality"? Eckhart leads us on a difficult path. He urges us not to treat the spirit/spirituality as a property or possession, as something we have or own in addition to our material, psychic, or mental possessions. He urges us to let go of all of that, to enter into a state of dispossession, of utter poverty or emptiness.

In his sermon Eckhart first speaks of two kinds of poverty, an outer and an inner poverty. "The first is an outer poverty," he says, "and that is good and very praiseworthy in those people who willingly take it upon themselves out of love for our Lord, because he too was poor in this sense while he was on earth." Eckhart speaks no further of this kind of poverty but instead turns to the other, the "inner poverty" that he considers more important. To introduce that kind, Eckhart briefly invokes the testimony of Albertus Magnus. "Bishop Albert," he states, "said that a poor person is one who takes no pleasure in any of the things God has ever created—and that is well said. However, I will say it still better and take poverty in a higher sense. A poor man is one who *wills* nothing, *knows* nothing, and *has* nothing." He then proceeds to speak of these three kinds of poverty.

Turning to *willing* nothing, Eckhart recognizes the difficulty of this notion for many people, especially for people who have "good intentions" and always want to do "good" by committing themselves to acts of penance and good works. Some people, he continues, go a step further by combining their willing with God's willing, saying that "a person must live so as not to fulfill his own will but strive to fulfill the will of God." Eckhart acknowledges that such people have made a "good beginning" because their intention seems laudable. Basically, however, they still "hold fast to their own selves which they consider to be great." Hence they are "neither poor nor similar to poor people." As he sternly adds: "They are considered great in the eyes of those who don't know any better. Yet I say they are asses and they don't understand anything of God's truth."

Pursuing this point, Eckhart indicates clearly what we have to let go or get rid of: "If someone asks me what that is (a poor person who *wills* nothing), I answer thus: As long as a person has something of himself which is his will with which he can will to fulfill the will of

God, such a person does not have the poverty of which we speak. For such a person still has a will with which he can satisfy the will of God, and that is not true poverty. For a person to have true poverty, he must be as empty of his created will as he was [empty] before he was [created]." Eckhart here makes a distinction between the ground (or un-ground) of all Being and the realm of created beings (which also includes God as a being and an object of desire). "Before the creatures were," he says, "God was not yet 'God'; he was rather what He was. As the creatures came into being and received their created being, God was no longer 'God in Himself' [but] rather was 'God' through and for creatures." This means that God after creation cannot be the highest goal of human desire or willing. Rather, humans must turn to the un-ground of Being and abandon separate willing. In Eckhart's stark language: "We pray that we may be free of 'God' [as object]," and a person poor in will must "will and desire as little as he willed and desired before he was [created]." In this way, the person who is poor "wills nothing."

As previously stated, in his sermon Eckhart extends the praise of emptiness also to *knowing* and *having* nothing. With regard to knowing, he exhorts us to get rid of all pretended knowledge, including knowledge of ourselves, of so-called eternal ideas, and even of God. A person who is genuinely poor in spirit, he says, must live as if "he does not even know that he lives, neither himself nor the 'truth' nor 'God.' Rather, he must be so empty of all knowledge that he neither knows nor recognizes nor senses that 'God' lives in him." Emptiness of knowing here means that a person "is as empty as he was when he was not yet [created] and allows God to act as He will." Once we have emptied ourselves into the groundless ground, we are robbed not only of our separate willing but also of knowing that God acts in the ground. Therefore, it is necessary for the poor person to desire to know or recognize *nothing* about his own work or the work of God. Only in this way can a person obtain poverty of knowing.

Finally, a person poor in willing and knowing also *has* or possesses nothing. Nonpossession here refers not only to material things but also and especially to spiritual things or matters of spirit. Eckhart calls this the supreme poverty, and its meaning is very radical. As he recognizes, there are people who say that a person should be completely free or empty of all things so that he or she can offer a place for God wherein God can work. Eckhart goes beyond that, saying: "If a person is empty of all things or beings, of himself and of God, yet if God can still find a place to work in him, that person is not poor in the truest sense." For God does not intend that person to have a place in himself where God can work; rather, it is true poverty of spirit when the person is "so empty of God and all His works, that God—if he wishes to work in the soul—is *Himself* [and nothing else] the place wherein He will work." If God finds a person that poor, God works His own works and the person "bears God within Himself . . . and thus is a pure God-bearer." Eckhart's sermon concludes with some bold and provocative statements of the sort for which he is so well known: "We say that the person must be so poor that he has no place in himself wherein God can work. Therefore, I pray that God will make me free of 'God' insofar as we take 'God' as beginning of all creation" (that is, of all created things and hence of all differentiation and separation).

This is the gist of the sermon *"Beati pauperes spiritu."* I had to abbreviate here and there. But even in its abbreviated form the message of the sermon is powerful; it is powerful in its indictment of human power, of a pretended human empowerment: the empowerment by God, by metaphysical knowledge, by eternal ideas and higher values. To avoid misunderstanding: the problem here is not God "as such" or eternal ideas and higher values "as such." The problem is their use and abuse for all too human initiatives, their instrumentalization for power or political agendas when human beings—specifically political elites—claim to be stand-ins for or "vice-regents" of God on earth. In human history this has happened all too often, especially in the history of Western imperialism. At the time of the Spanish conquest of America, the eminent historian Ginés de Sepulveda justified the conquest on the basis of both religion and philosophy, saying that both sanction the rule of "virtue over vice," of the civilized over the barbarian. The conquest resulted in the deaths of some seventy million native inhabitants by killing, starvation, and disease.

In subsequent history, imperial rule was justified less often by religion and more in terms of "civilization," a broad concept including a whole range of higher values and beliefs. In this context, it is good to remember some words of the Mahatma Gandhi, who struggled against the British Empire all his life. At the time of a visit to England, Gandhi was asked by reporters what he thought of Western civilization—to which he pithily replied: "It *would be* a good idea," meaning that there was much rhetoric but little or no substance.

The rhetoric of self-congratulation has continued unabated since Gandhi's time. Treated in this fashion, civilization is clearly "full of itself," full of its importance and the superiority of its values, including its "spiritual" values. Again, the point is not simply to debunk values, including spiritual values. The point is to abandon the claim of ownership or possession, a claim that would enable a person (or group of persons) to "know" these values fully and to "will" them by enacting and enforcing them on the rest of the world. The gospel of Luke lists not only a series of benedictions but also a series of maledictions or warnings: "Woe to you that are full now, for you shall hunger. Woe to you that are rich, for you have received your reward already. Woe to you when all men [especially the rulers and owners of the world] speak well of you." So the gospel praises not "*beati possidentes*" but rather "*beati pauperes*" and "*beati esurientes,*" "those who hunger and thirst." These blessings, of course, concur entirely with the words of Mary in her response to Gabriel (Luke 1:51–53): "[The Lord] has scattered the proud in the imagination of their hearts; he has put down the mighty from their thrones, and exalted those of low degree; he has filled the hungry (*esurientes*) with good things, and the rich he has sent away empty."

Here is a question for today, inspired by Luke's warnings: How long do the rulers of the earth believe they can own, dominate, and exploit the world without retribution? How long do they think they can, without retribution, delay or prevent the coming of the promise: the promise of peace with justice? How long?

Notes

Preface

1. J. Matthew Ashley, "Contemplation in Prophetic Action: Oscar Romero's Challenge to Spirituality in North America," in *Monseñor Oscar Romero: Human Rights Apostle* (Notre Dame, IN: Helen Kellogg Institute, 2000), 25, 30.

2. Martin Heidegger, *Nietzsche*, vol. 2 (Pfullingen, Germany: Neske, 1961), 391–92.

Introduction

1. Friedrich Nietzsche, "Thus Spoke Zarathustra," in *The Portable Nietzsche*, ed. Walter Kaufmann (New York: Viking Press, 1968), 417. See also Hannah Arendt, "Epilogue," in *The Promise of Politics*, ed. Jerome Kahn (New York: Schocken Books, 2005), 201.

2. According to one recent account: "The wilderness is the Old Testament metaphor for a covenantal social order. The Exodus narrative tells the story of Israel's leaving Pharaoh's Egypt. The Israelites went into the wilderness, a place where there were no viable life support systems; its only virtue was that it was beyond the reach of Pharaoh. What they discovered, according to the narrative, is that when they went into the desolate place, it turned out to have the life supports of bread as manna, water from rock, and meat from quail. It turned out that the wilderness was presided over by the gift-and-life-giving God." See Peter Block, Walter Brueggemann, and John McKnight, *The Other Kingdom: Departing the Consumer Culture* (Hoboken, NJ: Wiley, 2016), 15–16.

3. See, in this context, John D. Caputo, *The Weakness of God: A Theology of the Event* (Bloomington: Indiana University Press, 2006), and also my "Theocracy as Temptation: Empire and Mindfulness," in *Mindfulness and Letting Be* (Lanham, MD: Lexington Books, 2014), 127–30.

4. Block, Brueggemann, and McKnight, *The Other Kingdom*, xiv, 16.

5. Alasdair MacIntyre, *After Virtue: A Study in Moral Theory*, 3rd ed. (Notre Dame, IN: University of Notre Dame Press, 2007), xvi, 263.

6. Giorgio Agamben, *The Highest Poverty: Monastic Rules and Form-of-Life*, trans. Adam Kotako (Stanford, CA: Stanford University Press, 2013), xiii, 131. To avoid the confusion of "use" with utilitarianism, I replace "use" above with the expression "use/practice." This is also in agreement with Agamben's meaning when he writes (141): "Use, from this perspective . . . could have defined . . . the monks' vital practice, their form-of-life." Regarding the deeper spiritual intent, he adds (143): "The specific eschatological character of the Franciscan message is not expressed in a new doctrine, but in a form of life through which the very life of Christ is made newly present in the world."

7. See especially Martin Heidegger, *Das Ereignis*, ed. Friedrich-Wilhelm von Herrmann, in *Gesamtausgabe*, vol. 71 (Frankfurt: Klostermann, 2009), 122–25, 163; see also my "Farewell and *Ereignis*: Beyond Hard Power and Soft Power," in *Against Apocalypse: Recovering Humanity's Wholeness* (Lanham, MD: Lexington Press, 2016), 87–98.

8. See, e.g., Charles M. Leslie, *Anthropology of Folk Religion* (New York: Vintage Books, 1960), and "Folk Religion," in *The Concise Oxford Dictionary of World Religions*, ed. John Bowker (Oxford: Oxford University Press, 2000).

9. See Raimon Panikkar, *Worship and Secular Man* (Maryknoll, NY: Orbis Books, 1973), 1–2.

10. See Thomas Merton, *New Seeds of Contemplation* (New York: New Directions, 1961), 1–3.

11. Ibid., 54–55.

12. Pope Francis, "Homily in Redipuglia, Italy," September 13, 2014, available at http://w2.vatican.va/content/francesco/en/homilies /2014/documents/papa-francesco_20140913_omelia-sacrario-militare -redipuglia.html.

One   Faithful Expectation

1. A prominent example of this revitalizing effort is Russell Re Manning, ed., *Retrieving the Radical Tillich* (New York: Palgrave Macmillan,

2015). However, almost all the chapters in that volume are written by theologians or professors of religious studies. As Manning points out in his "Introduction," the effort is mainly to show Tillich's relevance to contemporary "radical theology" (from "death of God" theology to postmodernism and beyond). But despite the "multi-systematic" character (7) of Tillich's thought, Manning admits (15), "There is too little work in radical theology that actually does engage with practical matters such as the realities of economic injustice, sexism, and racism." Hence there is a "disjunction between theory and practice in the majority of radical theology."

2. As Ronald H. Stone notes, in 1918, in the immediate aftermath of World War I, Tillich "signed a statement by one of the minor groups supporting the separation of church and state." See his *Paul Tillich's Radical Social Thought* (Atlanta: John Knox Press, 1980), 40. Regarding the "healing" quality of the gospels, compare Tillich's statement: "Because the Christian message is the message of salvation and because salvation means healing, the message of healing in every sense of the word is appropriate to our situation." See "Aspects of a Religious Analysis of Culture," in *The Essential Tillich*, ed. F. Forrester Church (Chicago: University of Chicago Press, 1999), 109.

3. Stone, *Paul Tillich's Radical Social Thought*, 42–43.

4. In Stone's perceptive interpretation: "The age of spirit (Joachim) and the classless society (Marx) are not to be thought of as final stages; they too are subject to criticism and transformation. . . . Fulfillment is found in the vertical dimension of history; on the horizontal level, fulfillment is always fragmentary." See *Paul Tillich's Radical Social Thought*, 50–51.

5. Unless otherwise noted, all emphasis in the book is provided by the authors quoted.

6. Tillich, "Basic Principles of Religious Socialism," in *Paul Tillich: Political Expectation*, ed. James Luther Adams (New York: Harper & Row, 1971), 58–61.

7. Ibid., 62–64, 66–68. As Tillich adds (72): "The theonomous goal is an attitude in which 'autonomous' forms, freed from sacramental [sacrilegious?] distortion, are in turn freed from those naturalistically demonic distortions that enter in to empty them, and are filled with the import of the Unconditional."

8. As Stone remarks: "The idea of *Kairos* would remain central to his philosophy of society, but later reflection on the class struggle and continuing discussion with social philosophers in Dresden and Frankfurt would produce a more *immanent* religious socialism and a more realistic political outlook." See *Paul Tillich's Radical Social Thought*, 53. (Note: Tillich moved from Berlin to Marburg in 1924, to Dresden and Leipzig in

1925, and to Frankfurt in 1929.) Stone refers to some important writings of the mid-1920s that reflect the more "realist" trend: "The Religious Situation of the Present Time" (1926; very critical of the antireligious "spirit of capitalist society"), and "Faithful Realism" (1927/28). Compare also Tillich, "Religious Socialism" (dating from 1930), where we read: "Religious socialism adopts the decisive intention of Marxist anthropology and radicalizes it by shedding those elements of Marxism that are derived from bourgeois materialism and idealism. . . . [It] stands fundamentally on the ground of Marx's analysis of capitalist society." See *Paul Tillich: Political Expectation*, ed. Adams, 46, 48.

9. Stone, *Paul Tillich's Radical Social Thought*, 64.

10. Paul Tillich, *The Socialist Decision*, trans. Franklin Sherman (Eugene, OR: Wipf and Stock, 2012), xxxi–xxxiv, xxxvi–xxxvii.

11. Ibid., 1–6.

12. As Tillich writes, somewhat provocatively (22): "The actual life of the Jewish nation, like the actual life of every nation, is by nature pagan. . . . In fact, the Old Testament writings are a continuous testimony to the struggle of prophetic Judaism against pagan, national Judaism. . . . The 'Jewish problem' can only be solved by a decisive affirmation of the prophetic attack on the dominion of the myth of origin and all thinking bound to space." Tillich, *The Socialist Decision*.

13. Tillich, *The Socialist Decision*, 23–24, 27, 42–44. Curiously, in discussing "political Romanticism," Tillich does not mention Carl Schmitt's book *Political Romanticism*, first published in 1919 and translated by Guy Oakes (Cambridge, MA: MIT Press, 1986), where the phrase basically designates a sentimental-aesthetic outlook. Curiously, Schmitt himself defended a "political conservatism" that in many ways corresponds to Tillich's "conservative Romanticism."

14. Tillich, *The Socialist Decision*, 47–49, 51–52, 69. As Tillich writes (99–100): The socialist movement is "the reaction of the element of the 'human' in the proletariat against the threat of total human subjugation because of economic objectification. . . . The proletariat and the bond of origin, therefore, are not in contradiction." As he emphasizes, seen as a potential, socialism is not just a party program or fixed panacea but rather a prophetic "expectation" (132): "Socialism, at least in principle, must look beyond itself and its own achievement of a new social order. Socialism is not the end (*telos*) of socialism's striving. . . . Expectation is always bound to the concrete, and at the same time transcends every instance of the concrete."

15. In Tillich's words (*The Socialist Decision*, 108): "Hegel's philosophy of history . . . is a faith in providence expressed in rational form. He vehemently opposed a demand that is alien to being, a morality that

violates life. . . . Hegel spoiled his own concept by identifying a particular form of being as the tangible fulfillment of Being." As he adds (109),
Marx preserved Hegel's opposition to alienation: "The promise of socialism grows out of the analysis of being itself." However, Marx often limited himself to the level of a "purely economic analysis." Still, some of his
writings anticipate the idea of rehumanization or a "real humanism." See
also in this context Max Horkheimer and Theodor W. Adorno, *Dialectic of Enlightenment*, trans. John Cumming (New York: Seabury Press,
1972); see also Adorno, *Negative Dialectics*, trans. E. B Ashton (New
York: Seabury Press, 1973).

16. Tillich, *The Socialist Decision*, 161. The motto of "Socialism or
Barbarism" had been used by Rosa Luxemburg during World War I in her
so-called Junius Pamphlet of 1916. The motto was later used by a group of
French intellectuals under the leadership of Cornelius Castoriadis. Com-
pare also Istvan Meszáros, *Socialism or Barbarism: From the "American
Century" to the Crossroads* (New York: Monthly Review Press, 2001).

17. Compare in this context Brian Donnelly, *The Socialist Emigré:
Marxism and the Later Tillich* (Macon, GA: Mercer University Press,
2003). Tillich was quite aware of his emigré status, which he considered a
religious experience. As he writes in his autobiography: "The command
to go from one's county is more often a call to break with ruling authorities and prevailing social and political patterns, and to resist them pas-
sively or actively. It is a demand for 'spiritual emigration,' the Christian
community's attitude toward the Roman Empire. . . . I began to be an
'emigrant' personally and spiritually long before I actually left my homeland." See Tillich, *On the Boundary: An Autobiographical Sketch* (New
York: Scribner's Sons, 1966), 92–93.

18. For a critique of Barthian "dialectical theory" see especially Tillich, "What Is Wrong with the Dialectic Theology" (1935), in *Paul Tillich: Theologian of the Boundaries*, ed. Mark K. Taylor (London: Collins,
1987), 104–16. On the derailments of faith through either politicization
or privatization, see my "Religion and the World: The Quest for Justice
and Peace," in my *Integral Pluralism: Beyond Culture Wars* (Lexington:
University Press of Kentucky, 2010), 85–104.

19. Tillich, *On the Boundary*, 83. Regarding Marxism he writes (85,
89): "I owe to Marx an insight into the ideological character not only of
idealism but also of all systems of thought, religious and secular, which
serve power structures and thus prevent, even if unconsciously, a more
just organization of reality. . . . But Marxism has not only an 'unmasking'
effect, it involves also a demand and expectation and, as such, it has had
and continues to have a tremendous impact on history." Regarding Schelling, compare Max Werner, *The Philosophy of F. W. J. Schelling: History,*

System, and Freedom, trans. Thomas Nenon (Bloomington: Indiana University Press, 1984); see also my "Nature and Spirit: Schelling," in my *Return to Nature: An Ecological Counter History* (Lexington: University Press of Kentucky, 2011), 33–52.

20. See Stephen Prothero, *American Jesus: How the Son of God Became a National Icon* (New York: Farrar, Straus and Giroux, 2003); R. Laurence Moore, *Selling God: American Religion in the Marketplace of Culture* (New York: Oxford University Press, 1994). See also William E. Connolly, *Capitalism and Christianity, American Style* (Durham, NC: Duke University Press, 2008).

21. See H. Richard Niebuhr, Wilhelm Pauck, and Francis Miller, *The Church against the World* (New York: Willet, Clark, 1935), 128. Compare also Tzvetan Todorov, *The Inner Enemies of Democracy*, trans. Andrew Brown (Cambridge: Polity Press, 2014), 29–77, especially 77: "Morality and justice placed at the service of state policy actually harm morality and justice, turning them into mere tools in the hands of the powerful. . . . Messianism, this policy carried out on behalf of the good and the just, does both a disservice."

22. See Tillich, "The Kingdom of God and History," in *The Kingdom of God and History*, ed. H. G. Wood et al. (Chicago: Willett, Clark, 1938), 116–17. As he states on the latter point (109): Religious socialism "starts with the insight that the bourgeois-capitalist epoch of Western development has reached the stage of a most radical transformation which may mean the end of that epoch altogether. . . . The religious interpretation of history has two roots—a religious-transcendent root, the Christian message of the Kingdom of God, and a political-immanent root, the socialist interpretation of the present. The former supplies the principles and criteria, the latter the material and concrete application. This bi-polar [dialectical] method is essential for any religious interpretation of history."

23. Tillich, "The Church and Communism," in *Religion in Life* 6: 3 (1937): 347, 350, 357.

24. See Tillich, *An meine deutschen Freunde* (Stuttgart: Evangelisches Verlagswerk, 1973); see also Ronald H. Stone and Matthew Lon Weaver, eds., *Against the Third Reich* (Louisville, KY: Westminster/John Knox Press, 1998).

25. See Tillich, *War Aims* (New York: Protestant Digest, 1941). In the words of Ronald Stone: "Tillich revealed his fears that, after the war, the Leviathan of an uncaring, monopolistic capitalism would be enforced on Europe. Capitalism in control of technology would foster the dehumanization process that nurtured Nazism. . . . [In his view] a new order would require transforming the present technical-rationalistic manipulation of the human world into a new political-spiritual reality. . . . He

expressed his fears that Europe would be reduced to a colonial hinter-
land of the emerging superpowers." See *Paul Tillich's Radical Social
Thought*, 106.

26. Tillich, "Protestant Principles," in *The Protestant* 4: 5 (April–
May 1942): 17–18. As Stone remarks perceptively: For Tillich "the essence
of Protestantism, or prophetic religion, is the dual recognition of the transcendence and immanence of God. All of life has a religious base, but life
itself is not divine. Religion has two senses: its special proclamation of its
vision of God, and the denial that its special proclamation is absolute."
See *Paul Tillich's Radical Social Thought*, 100.

27. As Tillich stated in "A Program for a Democratic Germany":
"Only through the cooperation between the Western powers and Russia
will it be possible to achieve the reconstruction of Europe which must
follow the necessary and certain defeat of Hitler Germany." See Ronald
Stone, ed., *Theology of Peace: Paul Tillich* (Louisville, KY: Westminster/
John Knox Press, 1990), 105. As Stone comments at another point regarding the Council: "What policy it had depended on a united Germany
and some cooperation between the U.S. and the USSR. With division and
antagonism, it had no program. With the imposition of military rule and
the return of monopoly capitalism [in West Germany] after the war, Tillich's dream of a liberating religious socialism had almost no chance for
realization." He also mentions that Tillich was "blacklisted by the U.S.
Army" for a while. See *Paul Tillich's Radical Social Thought*, 108.

28. Tillich, "The World Situation" (1945), in *Theology of Peace*, ed.
Stone, 112.

29. Ibid., 116, 118, 132–33, 138.

30. Ibid., 136, 156.

31. See in this context Tillich, *Christianity and the Encounter of the
World Religions* (New York: Columbia University Press, 1963); see also
Jeffrey Small, *God as the Ground of Being: Tillich and Buddhism in Dia-
logue* (Cologne, Germany: Lambert Academic Publishing, 2009).

32. As Stone writes: "During the presidency of Dwight D. Eisen-
hower (1953–60), Tillich was less politically active than before as he
pushed to finish his *Systematic Theology*. . . . Nonetheless, he endorsed
the candidacy of John F. Kennedy and was present at his inauguration. . . .
The news of Kennedy's assassination in November 1963 reached him
while he was in Europe and saddened him deeply." See Stone's "On the
Boundary of Utopia and Politics," in *The Cambridge Companion to Paul
Tillich*, ed. Russel Re Manning (Cambridge: Cambridge University Press,
2009), 216.

33. Tillich, *Systematic Theology*, vol. 3: *Life and the Spirit: History
and Kingdom of God* (Chicago: University of Chicago Press, 1963).

34. Ibid., 357, 361, 363, 377.

35. Ibid., 397, 399.

36. See Tillich, *The Christian Conscience and Weapons of Mass Destruction* (New York: Federal Council of Churches in America, 1950).

37. See Tillich, "The Hydrogen Bomb," in *Theology of Peace*, ed. Stone, 158–59. In his *Paul Tillich's Radical Social Thought*, Stone provides some historical background to this statement (125–26), indicating that it was published in the *New York Times* on November 15, 1957, and again used by SANE in 1961. Stone also mentions some of Tillich's other public activities in the last years of his life (127): "He threw his efforts behind a group working to repeal the McCarran (Immigration and Nationality) Act. He signed statements calling for the abolition of the House Un-American Activities Committee. He lent the use of his name to groups promoting civil rights for blacks. He joined Donald M. Fraser's committee working for open housing in 1965 . . . [He] joined other religious leaders in urging caution during the Cuban missile crisis."

38. Tillich, *The Shaking of the Foundations* (New York: Charles Scribner's Sons, 1948), 2–3.

39. Ibid., 6–7, 9–11.

40. Compare in this context my *Against Apocalypse: Recovering Humanity's Wholeness* (Lanham, MD: Lexington Books, 2016).

41. Stone, "On the Boundary of Utopia and Politics," 219. As Stone adds (219–20): "His is a testimony of personal religious solace grounded in love, action and moments of religious experience. His political outlook was critical and restless: his critique of the pretensions of National Socialism drove him out of Germany, and his critique of American oligarchic rule, nuclear defense policies, foreign policy towards Germany and militarism gained him the enmity of the FBI and regressive forces in the United States." Compare also Francis Ching-Wah Yip, *Capitalism as Religion? A Study of Paul Tillich's Interpretation of Modernity* (Cambridge, MA: Harvard Theological Studies, 2010), which discusses Tillich's "critique of capitalist modernity," pointing to affinities of this critique with the early Frankfurt School. The book also seeks to "update" Tillich's work from the angle of the ongoing process of globalization.

Two   Sacred Secularity

1. See Raimon Panikkar, *The Rhythm of Being: The Gifford Lectures* (Maryknoll, NY: Orbis Books, 2010). Compare also my "A Secular Age? Reflections on Taylor and Panikkar," in my *Being in the World:*

Dialogue and Cosmopolis (Lexington: University Press of Kentucky, 2015), 119–50.

2. See Panikkar, *Worship and Secular Man* (Maryknoll, NY: Orbis Books, 1973), 1–2. Regarding Paul Tillich, compare his "Basic Principles of Religious Socialism," in his *Political Expectation* (New York: Harper & Row, 1971), 38–88.

3. Panikkar, *Worship and Secular Man*, 7, 10–13.

4. Ibid., 18, 20–22. On the "ek-static" character of human existence, see especially Martin Heidegger, "Letter on Humanism" (1946), in *Heidegger: Basic Writings*, ed. David F. Krell (New York: Harper & Row, 1977), 203–7. On symbolism, compare Mircea Eliade, *Images and Symbols: Studies in Religious Symbolism*, trans. P. Mairet (London: Harvill Press, 1961).

5. Panikkar, *Worship and Secular Man*, 28–30, 33–36. Regarding the notion of the "profane" (as an antireligious category), compare Mircea Eliade, *The Sacred and the Profane: The Nature of Religion*, trans. W. Trask (London: Harcourt Brace Jovanovich, 1959).

6. Panikkar, *Worship and Secular Man*, 42, 47, 49–52. See also his book *The Cosmotheandric Experience*, ed. Scott Eastham (Maryknoll, NY: Orbis Books, 1993).

7. Panikkar, "Religion or Politics: The Western Dilemma," in *Religion and Politics in the Modern World*, ed. Peter H. Merkl and Ninian Smart (New York: New York University Press, 1983), 44–47, 49–50. The article offers some helpful definitions. Distantly echoing Aristotle, politics is said to denote "the sum total of principles, symbols, means and actions" whereby humans endeavor to attain "the *common good of the polis*." On the other hand, religion is said to refer to "the sum total of principles, symbols, means and actions" whereby humans expect to reach "the *summum bonum* of life." Differently phrased, politics is concerned with "the realization of a human order," while religion aims at "the realization of the ultimate order" (where the latter phrase seems to resonate with what Tillich has called "ultimate concern").

8. Panikkar, *The Intra-Religious Dialogue* (New York: Paulist Press, 1978), xiv–xix.

9. Ibid., xxvii, 50, 91. (In the previous presentation I have tried to correct for Panikkar's frequent use of the term "Man.") The importance of dialogical pluralism is also stressed in Panikkar's book *A Dwelling Place for Wisdom*, where he remarks that, with regard to the diversity of religious traditions, "the time has come for a pluralistic attitude—for a head-first dive into the Ganges." As he elaborates again, "genuine pluralism is not equivalent to factual plurality or multiplicity but involves an ethical engagement with religious difference." Invoking Indian terminology, he

adds that pluralism entails "a nondualist, *advaitic* attitude which defends truth's pluralism since truth itself is pluralistic" and "cannot be expressed in terms of either unity or multiplicity." See *A Dwelling Place for Wisdom*, trans. Annemarie S. Kidder (Louisville, KY: Westminster/John Knox Press, 1993), 146–47. For a critique of Panikkar's pluralism, compare Gerald J. Larson, "Contra Pluralism," in *The Intercultural Challenge of Raimon Panikkar*, ed. Joseph Prabhu (Maryknoll, NY: Orbis Books, 1996), 71–87.

   10. Panikkar, *The Intra-Religious Dialogue*, 3, 15, 61. A similar argument was extended to the strictly philosophical domain in Panikkar's important essay "What Is Comparative Philosophy Comparing?," in *Interpreting across Boundaries: New Essays in Comparative Philosophy*, ed. Gerald J. Larson and Elict Deutsch (Princeton, NJ: Princeton University Press, 1988), 116–36.

   11. Panikkar, "The Invisible Harmony: A Universal Theory of Religion or a Cosmic Confidence in Reality?," in *Toward a Universal Theology of Religion*, ed. Leonard Swidler (Maryknoll, NY: Orbis Books, 1987), 119–20. Regarding the "end of history," see Francis Fukuyama, *The End of History and the Last Man* (New York: Free Press, 1992).

   12. Panikkar, "The Invisible Harmony," 121–22. Compare in this context also Alan Sheridan, *Michel Foucault: The Will to Truth* (London: Tavistock Publications, 1980).

   13. Panikkar, "The Invisible Harmony," 125, 127, 138–40.

   14. Ibid., 141–43. For arguments along similar lines, compare also Panikkar, "The Jordan, the Tiber, the Ganges: Three Kairological Moments of Christic Self-Consciousness," in *The Myth of Christian Uniqueness: Toward a Pluralistic Theology of Religion*, ed. John Hick and Paul F. Knitter (Maryknoll, NY: Orbis Books, 1987), 89–116.

   15. Panikkar, *Cultural Disarmament: The Way to Peace*, trans. Robert R. Barr (Louisville, KY: Westminster John Knox Press, 1995), 9–10, 33. Compare also my *Peace Talks—Who Will Listen?* (Notre Dame, IN: University of Notre Dame Press, 2004).

   16. Panikkar, *Cultural Disarmament*, 15–19, 64–74.

   17. Ibid., 17, 19–20, 25, 29. As Panikkar elaborates (29): "World War II and the American war in Vietnam can serve as examples of wars that are not explicitly religious but that nevertheless have a religious character. They had a religious *ethos*: the rescue of Civilization, Freedom, Democracy, all with capital letters." On the millenarian character of *pax Americana*, compare Tzvetan Todorov, *The Inner Enemies of Democracy*, trans. Andrew Brown (Cambridge: Polity, 2014), especially his comment (58) that "American policy tips over from the universal principle of

self-defense into the messianism which leads the U.S. to believe it has the task of saving humanity."

18. Panikkar, *Cultural Disarmament*, 34–35, 80–92. Compare in this context Richard Falk and David Krieger, eds., *At the Nuclear Precipice: Catastrophe or Transformation?* (New York: Palgrave Macmillan, 2008), and my book *Against Apocalypse: Recovering Humanity's Wholeness* (Lanham, MD: Lexington Books, 2016).

19. Panikkar, *Cultural Disarmament*, 22–23, 83, 88, 94.

20. Ibid., 65. See Dante, *Divina Comedia, Inferno* III, 5–6. For Heidegger's invocation of Hölderlin's phrase, compare his "The Question Concerning Technology," in *Heidegger: Basic Writings*, ed. David F. Krell (New York: Harper & Row, 1977), 310, 316.

21. For the reference to fullness or *pleroma*, see Panikkar, *The Intra-Religious Dialogue*, 82. Regarding the ultimate anchoring of hope or promise in reality or some sense of "being," compare his following statements (which are not incompatible with Tillich's teachings): "Peace can only be a harmony of the very reality in which we share when we find ourselves in a situation of receptiveness by virtue of not having placed obstacles in the way of the rhythm of reality, of the Spirit, of the ultimate structure of the universe. . . . In the last analysis, only that which *is* [ontologically] enables us to measure, think, judge *what* is. What *has to be* is subordinate to that which *is*. But this *is*, understood as synonymous with *being*, also means *becoming* and *'oughting' to be*." See Panikkar, *Cultural Disarmament*, 10, 14.

22. Panikkar, *Cultural Disarmament*, 91. See also Paul Knitter, "Cosmic Confidence or Preferential Option?," in *The Intercultural Challenge of Raimon Panikkar*, ed. Joseph Prabhu (Maryknoll, NY: Orbis Books, 1996), 187, 189, 195. In a critical vein, Knitter invokes the suspicion of David Tracy that holistic pluralism can easily lead to the temptation "to enjoy the pleasure of difference without ever committing oneself to any particular vision of resistance or hope." See Tracy, *Plurality and Ambiguity: Hermeneutics, Religion, Hope* (New York: Harper & Row, 1987), 90.

23. Panikkar, "A Self-Critical Dialogue," in *The Intercultural Challenge of Raimon Panikkar*, ed. Prabhu, 276–77, 281–83. As he adds (281): "The Vedic notion *rta* or cosmic order may be a homeomorphic equivalent of what we are saying."

24. Panikkar, *Blessed Simplicity: The Monk as Universal Archetype* (New York: Seabury Press, 1982), 10–12, 14.

25. Ibid., 98. Compare also my book *Mindfulness and Letting-Be: On Engaged Thinking and Acting* (Lanham, MD: Lexington Books, 2014).

26. Panikkar, *Blessed Simplicity*, 16.

Three   From Desert to Bloom

1. Joan Baez, in *Merton: By Those Who Knew Him Best*, ed. Paul Wilkes (San Francisco: Harper & Row, 1984), 43. See also Raimon Panikkar, *Blessed Simplicity: The Monk as Universal Archetype* (New York: Seabury Press, 1982), 16–17, and Alfred Camus, *The Rebel: An Essay on Man in Revolt*, trans. Anthony Bower (New York: Vintage Books, 1956).

2. William H. Shannon, *Something of a Rebel: Thomas Merton, His Life and Works, An Introduction* (Cincinnati: St. Anthony Messenger Press, 1997), xi–xiii.

3. Thomas Merton, *The Wisdom of the Desert* (New York: New Directions Publishing, 1960), 23. As he states there (23): "The Coptic hermits who left the world as though escaping from a wreck, did not merely intend to save themselves. They knew that they were helpless to do any good for others as long as they floundered around in the wreckage. But once they got a foothold on solid ground, things were different. Then they had not only the power but even the obligation to pull the whole world to safety after them. . . . We must liberate ourselves, in our own way, from involvement in a world that is plunging into disaster."

4. Merton, *The Straits of Dover*, unfinished novel, cited by Shannon, *Something of a Rebel*, 16.

5. Merton, *Seeds of Contemplation* (New York: New Directions, 1949), 17. In Shannon's words: "Discovering one's own inner depths and finding God there is not just a monastic endeavor; it is a human one." *Something of a Rebel*, 71–72.

6. Merton, *New Seeds of Contemplation* (New York: New Directions, 1961), 1–3. As he adds (5): Contemplation is "awakening, enlightenment, and the amazing intuitive grasp by which love gains certitude of God's creative and dynamic intervention in our daily life."

7. See, e.g., Merton, *The Road to Joy: Letters to New and Old Friends*, ed. Robert E. Daggy (New York: Farrar, Straus and Giroux, 1989), 118; compare also Shannon, *Something of a Rebel*, 67–69.

8. Merton, *New Seeds of Contemplation*, 8–10.

9. Ibid., 52–55. Compare in this context also *Entering the Silence: The Journals of Thomas Merton*, vol. 2, ed. Jonathan Montaldo (San Francisco: HarperCollins, 1997).

10. Merton, *New Seeds of Contemplation*, 12–13. The "is" here refers to "Being" and to the epithet of God as the "I am" (13): "There is 'no such thing' as God because God is neither a 'What' nor a 'thing' but a pure 'Who.' . . . He is the 'I am' before whom with our own most personal and inalienable voice we echo 'I am'."

11. Shannon, *Something of a Rebel*, 73. According to Shannon, the poem was written around 1949.

12. Shannon, *Something of a Rebel*, 173. In his words (174): "Merton, for me, is one of the great prophets of our time and perhaps for generations to come."

13. Merton, *Conjectures of a Guilty Bystander* (Garden City, NY: Doubleday, 1966), 156, 158. As Shannon comments (in *Something of a Rebel*, 35): Contemplation taught Merton "that in finding God he had found God's people and he had found them in God." Shannon is one of the commentators who finds a hiatus between the younger and the older Merton: "Between 1955 and 1965 Merton became a very different kind of monk from the one who had in 1941 entered Gethsemani with the fervent desire to leave the world behind and give himself to God alone. . . . [What he discovered was that] the world is on both sides of the monastic walls." *Something of a Rebel*, 35–37. The phrase "letting-be" is, of course, a vintage Heideggerian phrase. See my "Agency and Letting-Be: Heidegger on Primordial Praxis," in my *The Promise of Democracy: Political Agency and Transformation* (Albany: State University of New York Press, 2010), 67–81.

14. Merton, *The Seven Storey Mountain* (New York: Harcourt Brace, 1948). The passage is actually contained in the Japanese edition of that work, reprinted in *Honorable Reader: Reflections on My Work*, ed. Robert E. Daggy (New York: Crossroad, 1989), 65–66.

15. Merton, *Contemplation in a World of Action* (1st ed. 1971; Notre Dame, IN: University of Notre Dame Press, 1995), 141–42.

16. Ibid., 143, 146–47. Compare also my *Being-in-the-World: Dialogue and Cosmopolis* (Lexington: University Press of Kentucky, 2014). Merton does not ignore the dangers involved in "worldly" action, especially the danger of falling prey to, or being co-opted by, all kinds of ideological agendas hostile to contemplation and reflection. He speaks in this context (147) of "empty stereotypes of world affirmation" in which he has "very little confidence."

17. Merton, *Conjectures of a Guilty Bystander* (New York: Doubleday, 1965), 5–7.

18. Ibid., 31–32. As he adds (33): "The result is likely to be very unpleasant, and the blame will rest squarely on the shoulders of White America, with its emotional, cultural and political immaturity and its pitiable refusal of insight."

19. Merton, *Conjectures of a Guilty Bystander*, 34–38.

20. Ibid., 263. The above statements can be compared with benefit with thoughts expressed by the Vietnamese Buddhist monk whom Merton admired greatly, Thich Nhat Hanh: "When fear becomes collective,

when anger becomes collective, it is extremely dangerous. It is over-whelming. . . . The mass media and the military-industrial complex cre-ate a prison for us, so we all continue to think, see, and act in the same way. . . . We need the courage to express ourselves even when the majority is going in the opposite direction." See *The Art of Power* (New York: HarperCollins, 2008), 12.

21. Merton, *Cold War Letters*, ed. Christine M. Bochen and William H. Shannon (Maryknoll, NY: Orbis Books, 2006), 130, 173–74. As James W. Douglass writes in his "Preface" (xvi): "The *Cold War Letters* are Thomas Merton at his best, writing to us at our collective worst." Com-pare also Edward Teller, *The Legacy of Hiroshima* (Garden City, NY: Doubleday, 1962), and my *Against Apocalypse: Recovering Humanity's Wholeness* (Lanham, MD: Lexington Books, 2016).

22. Merton, *Cold War Letters*, 46, 129.

23. Ibid., 38, 43–44. As he adds in his letter to the fellow priest (36): Among political leaders there seems to be "no alternative to a policy based on this threat of nuclear extermination. . . . One does not have to have the explicit intention of becoming a war criminal in order to become one. One just has to do what is flagrantly unjust and wrong, no matter for what good end." And in a letter to Ethel Kennedy we find these lines (27–28): "As a nation we have begun to float into a moral void and all the sermons of all the priests in the country (if they preach at all) are not going to help much." In the same letter there is also the statement, particularly relevant in our "second" Cold War: "Every form of healthy human contact with Russia and above all China is to be encouraged. We have got to see each other as *people* and not as demons."

24. Merton, *Cold War Letters*, 21–22, 129. Another glimpse of his broad, nonsectarian humanism can be found in a letter to Arthur Miller (169): "I must read Emerson. . . . Thoreau, of course, I admire tremen-dously. He is one of the only reasons why I felt justified in becoming an American citizen. He and Emily Dickenson, and some of my friends and people like yourself. It is to me a great thing that you say I am like the [New England] transcendentalists [many of whom were Unitarians]. I will try to be worthy of that."

25. Merton, ed., *Gandhi on Non-Violence* (New York: New Direc-tions Publishing, 1965), 3–4. As he adds (4): "The West has not been able to listen to the East, to Africa, and to the now practically extinct voice of primitive America. As a result of this, the ancient wisdoms have them-selves fallen into disrepute and Asia no longer dares listen to herself."

26. Merton, *Gandhi on Non-Violence*, 6–8. Regarding creative trans-formation he adds (9): "In discovering India and his own 'right mind,' Gandhi was not excavating from libraries the obscure disputed questions

of Vedantic scholasticism (though he did not reject Vedanta). He was, on the contrary, identifying himself fully with the Indian people, that is to say, not with the Westernized upper classes nor with the Brahmin caste, but rather with the starving masses and in particular with the outcaste 'untouchables' or *Harijans*." Compare in this context my "Homecoming through Otherness," in my *The Other Heidegger* (Ithaca, NY: Cornell University Press, 1993), 149–80, and also my "Homelessness and Pilgrimage: Heidegger on the Road," in my *Peace Talks—Who Will Listen?* (Notre Dame, IN: University of Notre Dame Press, 2004), 192–204.

27. Merton, *Gandhi on Non-Violence*, 9–10, 12–13. Tellingly, Merton in this context invokes the work of Hannah Arendt with her emphasis on language, the "public sphere," and a critique of violence. See Arendt, *The Human Condition: A Study of the Central Dilemmas Facing Modern Man* (Chicago: University of Chicago Press, 1958), and also my "On Violence: Post-Arendtian Reflections," in my *Peace Talks—Who Will Listen?*, 111–31.

28. Merton, *Gandhi and Non-Violence*, 16–17.

29. Merton, *Cold War Letters*, 42, 126.

30. Merton, *Mystics and Zen Masters* (New York: Noonday Press, 1964), 14, 17. As he writes at another point: "To approach the subject of Zen with an intellectual or theological chip on the shoulder would end only in confusion." See Merton, *Zen and the Birds of Appetite* (New York: New Directions, 1965), 33.

31. Merton, *The Asian Journal* (New York: New Directions Books, 1968), 4. According to Shannon, one of the friends who drove him to the airport reported: "Tom was as excited as a little kid on his first trip to Disneyland." See *Something of a Rebel*, 165.

32. Merton, *The Asian Journal*, 308, 313. The notes for the Calcutta talk are followed by more general reflections in "Monastic Experience and East-West Dialogue" (309–17), reflections that still deserve close attention from all students of East-West dialogues and encounters.

33. For the earlier account see Merton, *The Asian Journal*, 101, 135–36, 257–58, 333–34.

34. Merton, *The Asian Journal*, 317. See also Shannon, *Something of a Rebel*, 49, 53–54, 93, 106. Compare Merton's statement in 1967 in a message from contemplatives to the "world": "My brother [and sister], perhaps in my solitude . . . I have been summoned to explore a desert area of man's heart in which explanations no longer suffice and in which one learns that only experience counts." See *The Hidden Ground of Love: The Letters of Thomas Merton on Religious Experience and Social Concerns*, ed. William H. Shannon (New York: Farrar, Straus and Giroux, 1985), 156.

Four   Herald of Glad Tidings

1. Pope Francis, "Homily in Redipuglia, Italy," September 13, 2014, available at http://www.zenit.org/en/articles/pope-francis-homily-at-the -world-war-i-memorial-in-redipuglia.

2. See Pope Francis, *The Joy of the Gospel: Evangelii Gaudium* (New York: Image, Random House, 2013).

3. See note 1.

4. Francis, *The Joy of the Gospel*, 42–43. One is reminded here of Marx's notion of *"lumpenproletariat."* One might also recall here Martin Heidegger's notion of *"Gestell,"* under whose aegis human beings are reduced to economic "resources" (*Menschenmaterial*).

5. Francis, *The Joy of the Gospel*, 44. For a critique of neoliberal economics, compare also Angus Sibley, *The "Poisoned Spring" of Economic Libertarianism* (Washington, DC: Pax Romana, 2011), and my "Market and Democracy: Beyond Neoliberalism," in my *Freedom and Solidarity: Toward New Beginnings* (Lexington: University Press of Kentucky, 2016), 79–95.

6. Francis, *The Joy of the Gospel*, 45–46, 51.

7. See "The Logic of Power and Violence," in Pope Francis, *The Church of Mercy: A Vision for the Church* (Chicago: Loyola Press, 2014), 111–12. The homily was presented at a prayer vigil for peace on September 7, 2013.

8. Francis, *The Church of Mercy*, 113–14. The audience was held on June 5, 2013. The chapter "Demolishing the Idols" attacks a few other personal or social derailments which cannot be discussed here: like the "leprosy of careerism" and the arrogance of self-centered "worldliness."

9. See "Pope Francis' Address to Congress." Video available at https://www.youtube.com/watch?v=oBM7DIeMsP0; transcript available at https://www.washingtonpost.com/local/social-issues/transcript -pope-franciss-speech-to-congress/2015/09/24/6d7d7ac8-62bf-11e5 -8e9e-dce8a2a2a679_story.html?utm_term=.4b0defce7a98.

10. See "Pope Francis' Remarks to the United Nations General Assembly," transcript available at http://www.nytimes.com/2015/09/26 /world/pope-francis-remarks-to-the-united-nations-general-assembly .html.

11. Francis, *The Joy of the Gospel*, 64–65.

12. Ibid., 175–76.

13. See note 10.

14. See note 9. The invocation of inspired leadership was also prominent in the pope's speech to the UN General Assembly. "I pay homage," he stated there, "to all those men and women whose loyalty and self-sacrifice

have benefited humanity as a whole in the past 70 years. In particular, I would recall today those who gave their lives for peace and reconciliation among peoples, from Dag Hammarskjöld to the many United Nations officials at every level who have been killed in the course of humanitarian missions, and missions of peace and reconciliation." See note 10.

15. See notes 9 and 10.

16. Francis, *The Joy of the Gospel*, 52–53, 134–35. Invoking an encyclical letter of Pope Paul VI, Francis adds (136): "We need to grow in a solidarity which 'would allow all peoples to become the artisans of their destiny,' since 'every person is called to self-fulfillment.'"

17. See Francis, "A Culture of Solidarity" and "For a New Solidarity" in his *The Church of Mercy*, 106–7, 129–30. Compare also my *Freedom and Solidarity*.

18. Francis, *The Joy of the Gospel*, 101–3, 171. Invoking an "apostolic exhortation" of Pope Paul VI, Francis (104) stresses the need to recognize that "the word is always beyond us, that 'we are not its masters or owners, but its guardians, heralds and servants.'" Regarding dialogue and the "word," see Hans-Georg Gadamer, *Truth and Method*, 2nd rev. ed., trans. Joel Weinsheimer and Donald G. Marshall (New York: Crossroad, 1989), part 2, 2, 405–38.

19. Francis, *The Joy of the Gospel*, 145, 161, 164, 166, 168. By counseling interfaith dialogue, the pontiff did not support a "facile syncretism." In his words (168), such a syncretism "would ultimately be a totalitarian gesture on the part of those who would ignore greater values of which they are not masters. True openness involves remaining steadfast in one's deepest convictions, clear and joyful in one's own identity."

20. Francis, *The Joy of the Gospel*, 55, 65–66, 125–26. The reference is to Pontifical Council of Justice and Peace, *Compendium of the Social Doctrine of the Church* (the Holy See: Libreria Editrice Vaticana, 2004; reprint 2005), 52.

21. Francis, *The Joy of the Gospel*, 152–60.

22. Ibid., 160, 172. The reference is to *Propositio* 55, which was adopted at the 13th Ordinary General Assembly of the Synod of Bishops gathered in Rome October 7–28, 2012.

23. Francis, *The Joy of the Gospel*, 128–29.

24. Ibid., 187.

Five   Modes of Religious Spirituality

1. In my view, the reason for this temporal phenomenon resides in the fact that our age is not only (or not primarily) a "secular age" but

a democratic or democratizing age in which divine "otherness" or transcendence needs to be accessible to people at large. One evidence of this trend, in Christianity, was Vatican II, but a similar trend can also be found in Islam, Hinduism, and Buddhism.

2. Compare, e.g., Martin Heidegger, *Das Ereignis*, ed. Friedrich-Wilhelm van Herrmann, *Gesamtaugabe*, vol. 71 (Frankfurt: Klosermann, 2009), 124–28.

3. Rudyard Kipling, "The Ballad of East and West," *The Pioneer*, December 2, 1889.

4. See Hans Küng and Karl-Josef Kuschel, eds., *A Global Ethic: The Declaration of the Parliament of the World's Religions* (New York: Continuum, 1995), 36. As Muller added, in a very "spirited" vein (101): "Religions and spiritual traditions: the world needs you very much! You, more than anyone else, have experience, wisdom, insights, and feelings for the miracle of life, of the earth, and of the universe. After having been sidelined in many fields of human endeavor, you must again be the lighthouse, the guides, the prophets and messengers of the one and final mysteries of the universe and eternity. You must set up the procedures to agree, and you must give humanity the divine or cosmic rules for behavior on this planet."

5. Regarding the meaning of "spirit" in different traditions see, e.g., "Soul, Spirit," in *The Perennial Dictionary of World Religions*, ed. Keith Grim et al. (San Francisco: Harper & Row, 1989), 699–702.

6. See Plato, *The Republic*, Book IV, 435b–441c. In modified form, the tripartition persists in Kant's three critiques and, still more recently, in the sociological (Weberian) distinction of the three "value spheres," science, ethics, and aesthetics (or art).

7. On the Chinese tradition of *hsin*, see especially William Theodore de Bary, *Neo-Confucian Orthodoxy and the Learning of the Mind-and-Heart* (New York: Columbia University Press, 1981).

8. See Philip Sheldrake, "What Is Spirituality?," in *Exploring Christian Spirituality: An Ecumenical Reader*, ed. Kenneth J. Collins (Grand Rapids, MI: Baker Books, 2000), 26–30. In Sheldrake's words (27), it would be most fruitful "to study the 'mysticism' of the Fathers as the very *heart of their theology*." Compare also Jordan Aumann, *Spiritual Theology* (London: Sheed and Ward, 1980).

9. Martin Luther, "The Freedom of a Christian," in *Martin Luther's Basic Theological Writings* (Minneapolis, MN: Fortress Press, 1989), 344–46. Compare also Bengt Hoffman, "Lutheran Spirituality," in *Exploring Christian Spirituality*, ed. Collins, 122–37.

10. Charles Taylor, *Sources of the Self: The Making of the Modern Identity* (Cambridge, MA: Harvard University Press, 1989), 512–13. From

an explicitly Christian perspective, Sheldrake writes: "I would suggest that what the word 'spirituality' seeks to express is the conscious human response to God that is both personal and ecclesial." See his "What Is Spirituality?," in *Exploring Christian Spirituality*, ed. Collins, 25. Compare also Karl Rahner's comments: "It has been said that the Christian of the future will be either a mystic or no longer a Christian. If we mean by mysticism not peculiar para-psychological phenomena but rather a genuine experience of God arising from the heart of existence, then the statement is correct and its truth and depth will become clearer in the spirituality of the future." See Rahner, "In Sorge um die Kirche," in his *Schriften zur Theologie*, vol. 14 (Einsiedeln, Switzerland: Benziger, 1960), 375.

11. As Wolfgang Böhme writes: "Christian mysticism [or spirituality] cannot be grounded entirely in 'inner' experience or reflect a pure inwardness. There must also be an impulse from beyond, an appeal in some kind of mundane form." See Böhme, ed., *Zu Dir Hin: Über mystische Lebenserfahrung, von Meister Eckhart to Paul Celan* (Frankfurt: Insel Verlag, 1987), 12. For further definitional clarifications, see Walter Principe, "Toward Defining Spirituality," in *Exploring Christian Spirituality*, ed. Collins, 43–59, and Alister E. McGrath, *Christian Spirituality: An Introduction* (Oxford: Blackwell, 1999). For a broader comparative perspective, see Eliot Deutsch, *Religion and Spirituality* (Albany: State University of New York Press, 1995).

12. In some versions of gnosticism, dualism or "dyotheism" is greatly attenuated in favor of an ascending scale of insight available to a select group. What links the various branches of gnosticism is mainly the stress on *"sophia"* or intellectual illumination leading to knowledge of the divine.

13. On gnostic traditions and teachings, see especially Hans Jonas, *The Gnostic Religion* (Boston: Beacon Press, 1963), and *Gnosis und spätantiker Geist*, 2 vols. (Göttingen: Vanderhoeck & Ruprecht, 1934–35); Gilles Quispel, *Gnosis als Weltreligion* (Zurich: Origo, 1951).

14. Occasionally there may be an odd combination of gnostic intellectualism and practical political engagement, with both addicted to monologue. Thus there can be a mixture of Cartesianism (centered in the knowing ego) and a dogmatic and monolithic Marxism (as some recent French philosophy reveals). Something like this may be behind Eric Voegelin's otherwise puzzling association of gnosticism with modern political mass movements. See his *Science, Politics and Gnosticism* (Chicago: Regnery, 1968). The possible connection between activist gnosticism and contemporary jihadism is mentioned in note 36.

15. The following presentation stays largely on an ecumenical level, thus bypassing denominational differences. For a discussion of

"Orthodox," "Anglican," "Methodist," "Evangelical," and similar forms of Christian spirituality, see *Exploring Christian Spirituality*, ed. Collins, part 3, 93–226.

16. Emil Brunner, *Die Mystik und das Wort* (Tubingen: Mohr, 1924), 387; cited in Böhme, *Zu Dir Hin*, 12.

17. At that time, Christian gnosticism often took the form of "docetism," a doctrine according to which Jesus was only seemingly human and his death on the cross only an apparent death but actually an illusion.

18. See Malcolm Barber, *The Trial of the Templars* (Cambridge: Cambridge University Press, 1994), 46; Trevor Ravenscroft and Tim Wallace-Murphy, *The Mark of the Beast* (London: Sphere Books, 1990), 53; Tim Wallace-Murphy and Marilyn Hopkins, *Rosslyn: Guardian of the Secrets of the Holy Grail* (Shaftesbury, UK: Element Books, 2000), 103–4.

19. Otto Uttendörfer, *Zinzendorfs religiöse Grundgedanken* (Herrnhut, Germany: Bruderhof, 1935), 161; cited in Dietrich Meyer, "Christus mein ander Ich: Zu Zinzendorfs Verhältnis zur Mystik," in *Zu Dir Hin*, ed. Böhme, 213.

20. In fact, the symbolism can be traced back even further to Jewish "wisdom" literature in which God and humankind were seen as linked in covenantal love.

21. Thomas à Kempis, *The Imitation of Christ* (New York: Penguin, 1952); also *De imitatione Christi* (Paris: Duprey, 1860), vol. 2, 38; cited by Josef Sudbrack in "Christliche Begegnungsmystik," in *Zu Dir Hin*, ed. Böhme, 142–43.

22. Gerhard Ebeling, *Die Wahrheit des Evangeliums* (Tubingen: Mohr, 1981), 207. Similarly Wolfgang Böhme observes: "Love is possible only when there is a Thou or You *toward* whom we can move, who addresses us, and with whom we can have a 'loving dialogue.' . . . Hence, the divine You remains the reference point, which militates against a [gnostic or pantheistic] submergence or disappearance in the cosmos [or in nothingness]." See Böhme, *Zu Dir Hin*, 11. Böhme also cites Martin Buber's rejection of a cosmic union or fusion which, for Buber, only reflected human conceit and self-aggrandizement; *I and Thou*, trans. Ronald G. Smith (Edinburgh: T & T Clark, 1958), 109–23.

23. For the passages from John of the Cross see Sudbrack, "Christliche Begegnungsmystik," in *Zu Dir Hin*, ed. Böhme, 146–48. As Sudbrack comments (148, 150): "There is here no fusion with the godhead, no expansion of consciousness to cosmic dimensions, no insinuation of ultimate convergence, nor any submergence in private subjectivity. . . . With indisputable clarity John of the Cross stresses the unbridgeable distance from God on the level of knowledge and sensation, while finding

a possible union only through active love." (I bypass here John's and Sudbrack's linkage of loving with "willing.") Compare also Marilyn M. Mallory, *Christian Mysticism—Transcending Techniques: A Theological Reflection on the Teaching of St. John of the Cross* (Amsterdam: Van Gorcum, 1977).

24. Teresa of Avila, *The Autobiography of St. Teresa of Avila* (Rockford, IL: Tan Books and Publishers, 1997), cited by Sudbrack in "Christliche Begegnungsmystik," 152–53. In Sudbrack's view (151, 153), it is impossible to understand Teresa's life and work without attention to the congruence of devotion to God and care for humans, of contemplation and commitment to social responsibility. Ultimately, the "encounter with Jesus" was for her the "touchstone" of spirituality. See also Sudbrack, *Erfahrung einer Liebe: Teresa von Avilas Mystik als Begegnung mit Gott* (Freiburg, Germany: Herder, 1979). One may compare Teresa's experience with Thomas Merton's turn from solitary contemplation to the "discovery" of people in his middle period.

25. Josef Zapf, "Die Geburt Gottes im Menschen: Nach Johannes Tauler," in *Zu Dir Hin*, ed. Böhme, 89. Compare also Georg Hofmann, ed., *Johannes Tauler: Predigten* (Einsiedeln, Switzerland: Johannes Verlag, 1979).

26. Dietrich Meyer, "Christus mein ander Ich," in *Zu Dir Hin*, ed. Böhme, 214–15, 217, 219. Zinzendorf's spirituality, in Meyer's words (225), involves "union with Christ as personal encounter and friendship." For Zinzendorf, this personal relation is primary, in contrast to any kind of "mystical fusion." Compare also Meyer, *Der Christozentrismus des späten Zinzendorf* (Bern, Switzerland: Herbert Lang, 1973).

27. For some philosophical discussion of Eckhart's thought, see Martin Heidegger, *Der Satz vom Grund* (Pfullingen, Germany: Neske, 1957), 71–74, and *Gelassenheit*, 2nd ed. (Pfullingen, Germany: Neske, 1970); John D. Caputo, *The Mystical Element in Heidegger's Thought* (Columbus: Ohio University Press, 1978).

28. Meister Eckhart, *Deutsche Predigten und Traktate*, ed. Josef Quint (Munich: Hanser, 1979), 53–57, 303–6, and *Meister Eckhart: The Essential Sermons, Commentaries, Treatises and Defenses*, trans. Edmund College and Bernard McGinn (New York: Paulist Press, 1981), 177–81, Sermon 2. For a discussion of the sermon *"Beati pauperes spiritu,"* see Otto Pöggeler, "Sein und Nichts: Mystische Elemente bei Heidegger und Celan," in *Zu Dir Hin*, ed. Böhme, 282–83; see also the epilogue.

29. Jacques Derrida, *Sauf le Nom* (Paris: Editions Galileé, 1993), 15–16, 31, 39, 76.

30. See Angelus Silesius, *Cherubinischer Wandersmann/Pélerin cherubinique* (Paris: Aubier, 1946). For the previous citations, see also

Alois M. Haas, "Christförmig sein: Die Christusmystik des Angelus Silesius," in *Zu Dir Hin*, ed. Böhme, 181–83, 185, 188. Haas relies on H. L. Held, *Angelus Silesius: Sämtliche Poetische Werke in drei Bänden* (Munich: Hanser, 1949–53).

31. Although rarely the target of *agape*, the Prophet himself is sometimes endowed with qualities of gnostic spirituality. A prominent example is this statement attributed to him: "I am an Arab without the letter *ayn* [i.e., a *rabb* or Lord]; I am Ahmad without the *mim* [mortality]; he who has seen me has seen the Truth." See the entry *"al-Insan al-Kamil"* ("the perfect man") in Cyril Glassé, ed., *The Concise Encyclopedia of Islam* (San Francisco: Harper Press, 1989), 189.

32. Cited in *The Concise Encyclopedia of Islam*, ed. Glassé, 168. (*Tarjumán al-Ashwaq* means "The Interpreter of Longings.") Among Ibn Arabi's most celebrated writings are *al-Futúhát al-Makkiyyah* ("The Meccan Revelations") and *Fusus al-Hikam* ("Bezels of Wisdom").

33. There is a sprawling literature surrounding Ibn Arabi's work. Compare especially Rom Landau, *The Philosophy of Ibn Arabi* (London: Allen and Unwin, 1959); Ibn al-Arabi, *Sufis of Andalusia* (Berkeley: University of California Press, 1972); Claude Addas, *Ibn Arabi; ou, La quête du soufre rouge* (Paris: Gallimard, 1989). In the Indian tradition, *"wahdat al-wujud"* can be broadly compared with a radical form of *Advaita Vedanta* according to which all finite beings are illusory and dissolved in the unity of *brahman*.

34. Ibn Arabi, *"Whoso Knoweth Himself . . . ,"* trans. T. H. Weir (Gloucesteshire, UK: Beshara Press, 1976), 4–5.

35. Ibid., 15, 20–23. A famous esoteric mystic who had claimed "I am God" long before Ibn Arabi was the Persian Husayn ibn Mansur, known as al-Hallaj (857–922). He was put to death by the Abbasid authorities in Baghdad.

36. See the entries on "Ismailis" and "Assassins" in *The Concise Encyclopedia of Islam*, ed. Glassé, 53–55, 194–200. In accordance with their dualistic doctrine, some Ismailis ascribed to the Prophet Muhammad a merely exoteric knowledge while crediting Ali (the fourth caliph and first Imam) with esoteric or "ineffable" knowledge. For a different and more favorable account, see Farhad Daftarg, *A Short History of the Ismailis* (Edinburgh: Edinburgh University Press, 1998), 15–16. The subterranean linkage of contemporary violent "jihadism" with the tradition of the "Assassins" is intriguing (but has not been sufficiently explored). On the purely contemplative level, one may note the connection between Islamic gnosticism and such newer intellectual developments as theosophy, exemplified by the work of Fritjof Schuon, especially his *Gnosis: Divine Wisdom*, trans. G. E. H. Palmer (London: John Murray, 1959). Profoundly

gnostic, in Ibn Arabi's vein, is this passage (77): "There are various ways of expressing or defining the difference between gnosis and love—or between *jñana* and *bhakti*—but here we wish to consider one criterion only, and it is this: for the 'volitional' or 'affective' man (the *bhakta*) God is 'He' and the ego is 'I,' whereas for the 'gnostic' or 'intellective' man (the *jñani*) God is 'I'—or 'Self'—and the ego is 'he' or 'other.'"

37. *The Essential Rumi*, trans. Coleman Barks, with John Moyne et al. (Edison, NJ: Castle Books), 21, 53, 131; see also the entry "Jalal ad-Din ar-Rumi" in Glassé, *The Concise Encyclopedia of Islam*, 205.

38. *The Essential Rumi*, 199; see also William C. Chittick, *The Sufi Path of Love: The Spiritual Teachings of Rumi* (Albany: State University of New York Press, 1983), 242.

39. See *The Essential Rumi*, 109, and Glassé, *The Concise Encyclopedia of Islam*, 205.

40. That social altruism may occasionally lead to a meddlesome manipulation of other lives can readily be acknowledged. However, it is possible to distinguish between such an attitude and a caring orientation that precisely respects and nurtures the freedom and integrity of others. See in this respect Martin Heidegger's distinction between a "managerial" care and an "anticipating-emancipatory" solicitude in *Being and Time*, trans. Joan Stambaugh (Albany: State University of New York Press, 1996), part 1, par. 26, 113–15. Compare also my *Freedom and Solidarity: Toward New Beginnings* (Lexington: University Press of Kentucky, 2015).

41. J. Matthew Ashley, "Contemplation in Prophetic Action: Oscar Romero's Challenge to Spirituality in North America," in *Monseñor Oscar Romero: Human Rights Apostle* (Notre Dame, IN: Helen Kellogg Institute for International Studies, 2000), 29.

42. See Wilder Foote, ed., *Servant of Peace: A Selection of the Speeches and Statements of Dag Hammarskjöld* (New York: Harper & Row, 1977), 24, 58. In this connection, one may also recall an address given by Czech President Václav Havel at Harvard University in 1996 under the title "A Challenge to Nourish Spiritual Roots Buried under Our Thin Global Skin." In that address Havel spoke of an "archetypal spirituality" implanted in humankind, beyond the confines of organized faiths, and "lying dormant in the deepest roots of most, if not all, cultures." See *Just Commentary* 28 (July 1996): 3.

Six   Emptiness and Compassion

1. Paul F. Knitter, *Without Buddha I Could Not Be a Christian* (Oxford: Oneworld, 2009).

2. Masao Abe, "Kenotic God and Dynamic Sunyata," in *The Emptying God: A Buddhist-Jewish-Christian Conversation*, ed. John B. Cobb Jr. and Christopher Ives (Maryknoll, NY: Orbis Books, 1990), 9–10, 14.

3. Ibid., 14, 19, 24. See also Karl Rahner, *Sacramentum Mundi* (London: Burns and Cates, 1969), vol. 2, 207; Jürgen Moltmann, *The Crucified God* (New York: Harper & Row, 1974), 204.

4. Abe, "Kenotic God and Dynamic Sunyata," 27–28. As he adds (27): "However important the notion of *sunyata* may be in Buddhism, following Martin Heidegger who put a cross mark 'X' on the term *Sein*, in order to show the unobjectifiability of *Sein*, we should also put a cross mark 'X' on *sunyata*."

5. Grace Cali, *Paul Tillich First Hand: A Memoir of the Harvard Years* (Chicago: Exploration Press, 1996), 72.

6. See Tillich, "A Dialogue between Paul Tillich and Hisamatsu Shin'ichi," in his *The Encounter of Religions and Quasi-Religions* (Lewiston, NY: Edwin Mellon, 1990), 140, 146, 148. Compare also Marc Boss, "Tillich in Dialogue with Japanese Buddhism," in *The Cambridge Companion to Paul Tillich*, ed. Russel Re Mannings (Cambridge: Cambridge University Press, 2009), 256–57, and Jeffrey Small, *God as the Ground of Being: Tillich and Buddhism in Dialogue* (Cologne, Germany: Lambert Academic Publishing, 2009).

7. For the comments in the "Informal Report" see Hannah Tillich, *From Place to Place* (New York: Stein & Day, 1976), 104–5. The comments on prayer were presented during a visit to Otain University in Kyoto, a center of Jodo Shin (or "Pure Land") Buddhism, which is more devotional than Zen. See Robert Wood, "Tillich Encounters Japan," in *Japanese Religions*, vol. 2, nos. 2–3 (1961–62): 53.

8. Tillich, "A Christian-Buddhist Conversation," in *Christianity and the Encounter of the World Religions* (New York: Columbia University Press, 1963), 2–3, 54, 62–63.

9. Ibid., 63–65.

10. Ibid., 70–73.

11. Ibid., 74–75. The conclusion of the chapter is puzzling in view of Tillich's own repeated transgression of Western "liberalism": for example, his championing of socialism (or the "socialist principle") as an antidote to capitalist selfishness and his articulation of "theonomy" as an alternative to both "autonomy" and "heteronomy." See, e.g., Tillich, *The Socialist Decision*, trans. Franklin Sherman (New York: Harper & Row, 1977); Tillich, *On the Boundary* (New York: Charles Scribner, 1966), 36–45.

12. Thomas Merton, "Preface," in his *Mystics and Zen Masters* (New York: Noonday Press, 1967), viii–x. For a comparison of Tillich and Merton, see Robert Giannini, "Paul Tillich and Thomas Merton: *Kairos* and

the Ascetic Life," in *Paul Tillich's Theological Legacy: Spirit and Community*, ed. Frederick J. Parrella (New York: De Gruyter, 1995), 142–48.

13. Merton, "The Other Side of Despair," in *Mystics and Zen Masters*, 263–65.

14. Merton, *Mystics and Zen Masters*, 266–67, 269. Merton transfers the notion of two kinds of community to the domains of organized religion (271–72): "We see the difference between two concepts of faith and of the Church. On the one hand, there is the idea that the Church is primarily an official and authoritative public organization. . . . [Here] the act of faith becomes a profession of orthodoxy and regularity, a protestation of conformity in order to merit, so to speak, a religious security clearance. . . . [Opposed to this stands the Church's calling] to disturb and unsettle believers in the world of facticity. . . . *Metanoiete*, repent, change your heart, is the inexhaustibly reported message of God's word to man in fallen society." Regarding the difficult relation between individual freedom and solidarity, see my *Freedom and Solidarity: Toward New Beginnings* (Lexington: University of Kentucky Press, 2015).

15. Merton, "Mystics and Zen Masters," in his *Mystics and Zen Masters*, 6–7, 13–14. Taking a leaf from the first Chinese Patriarch, Bodhidharma, Merton adds (17) that Zen consists "in a direct grasp of 'mind' or one's 'original face,'" but a grasp in which "one arrives at mind by 'having no mind' (*wu h'sin*), in fact, by 'being' mind instead of 'having' it." Differently put: Zen insight is "at once a liberation from the limitations of the individual ego and a discovery of one's 'original nature'"; basically, it is "not *our* awareness, but Being's awareness of itself in us."

16. Merton, "Mystics and Zen Masters," 20–23, 31.

17. Ibid., 24–27. As Merton adds (28, 34): "*Prajña* is not attained when one reaches a deeper interior center in one's self. . . . It does not consist in self-realization as an affirmation of one's own limited being, or as fruition of one's inner spiritual essence; on the contrary, it is liberated from any need of self-affirmation or self-realization whatever. . . . The mind that is emptiness, void, and *sunyata* is the *prajña*-mind."

18. Merton, "Mystics and Zen Masters," 25–26, 30.

19. Ibid., 31, 39–41. Merton (31) also calls the breakthrough an "apophatic" disclosure—which distantly resonates with Tillich's concept of "*kairos*" and Heidegger's notion of *Ereignis*.

20. Merton, "Buddhism and the Modern World," in *Mystics and Zen Masters*, 282–83. The chapter (284) refers briefly to Tillich's *Christianity and the Encounter of World Religions*, but without commentary.

21. Merton, "Buddhism and the Modern World," 284, 286.

22. Ibid., 286–87. As Merton pinpoints Nhat Hanh's approach (287): "A radical renewal of the Buddhist experiential grasp of reality within

the framework and context of a bitter agonizing social struggle, and in terms that are comprehensible to those who are most deeply involved in that struggle." This approach differs radically from Western designs of "regime change" guided by the "will to transform others." Compare also in this context Christopher S. Queen and Sallie B. King, eds., *Engaged Buddhism: Buddhist Liberation Movements in Asia* (Albany: State University of New York Press, 1996).

23. Raimon Panikkar, *The Silence of God: The Answer of the Buddha* (Maryknoll, NY: Orbis Books, 1982; first published in 1970 in Madrid). As he writes there (xxv–xxvi): "A larger part of today's humanity lives under the impression that some inescapable dialectic is at work between the ideologies of the First and Second Worlds. No wonder that violence and war seem inevitable. . . . [What is at the root is] the absurdity of two military superpowers playing at an ideo-theological war that threatens the very life of the planet. . . . The twin ideologies struggling today for the hegemony of the world and of consciences represent the last phases of a historical dialectic that, unless it is transcended by the contributions of other human cultures, will end by destroying history itself." As he adds, this is the "*Sitz im Leben*" (locus in life) of his book.

24. Panikkar, *The Silence of God*, 3, 5, 7, 14.

25. Ibid., 92, 94, 96.

26. Ibid., 96–97, 107. As he adds (117): "God is neither the Other, the distant, the extraneous, nor the One, the identical, the undivided. . . . God is neither altogether transcendent nor perfectly immanent. Neither dualism nor monism does justice to the divine mystery." Compare also Panikkar, *The Cosmotheandric Experience*, ed. Scott Eastham (Maryknoll, NY: Orbis Books, 1993).

27. Panikkar, *The Silence of God*, 129–31, 133. In all these statements one can, of course, notice the echo of Heidegger's emphasis on the withdrawal or sheltering of the divine. See, e.g., Heidegger, "Poetically Man Dwells . . . ," in his *Poetry, Language, Thought*, trans. Albert Hofstadter (New York: Harper & Row, 1971), 226–27; Jean Beaufret et al., *Heidegger et la question de Dieu* (Paris: Grasset, 1980). Compare Gianni Vattimo, *After Christianity*, trans. Luca D'Isanto (New York: Columbia University Press, 2002); John D. Caputo, *The Weakness of God: A Theology of the Event* (Bloomington: Indiana University Press, 2006); Richard Kearney, *The God Who May Be: A Hermeneutics of Religion* (Bloomington: Indiana University Press, 2001); and Kearney, *Anatheism: Returning to God after God* (New York: Columbia University Press, 2010).

28. Panikkar, *The Silence of God*, 161–64, 174.

29. Ibid., 174–76.

30. Compare in this context my "*Sunyata* East and West: Emptiness and Global Democracy," in my *Beyond Orientalism: Essays on Cross-Cultural Encounter* (Albany: State University of New York Press, 1996), 175–99, and my "Liberation Perspectives East and West," in my *Alternative Visions: Paths in the Global Village* (Lanham, MD: Rowman & Littlefield, 1998), 71–103.

Epilogue

1. Meister Eckhart, *The Essential Sermons, Commentaries, Treatises and Defenses*, trans. Edmund College and Bernard McGinn (New York: Paulist Press, 1981), 177–82, Sermon 2.

Index

Fred Dallmayr is Packey J. Dee Professor Emeritus in philosophy and political science at the University of Notre Dame. He is the author of *Peace Talks—Who Will Listen?* (University of Notre Dame Press, 2005), *In Search of the Good Life* (2007), and *Mindfulness and Letting Be* (2014).

CPSIA information can be obtained
at www.ICGtesting.com
Printed in the USA
LVOW13*2145101017
551932LV00003B/6/P